THROUGH THE EYES OF A COACH

THE NEW VISION FOR

Parenting
Leading
Loving
&Living

Cindy!
Bo!
WOO!
Joy to you
Fun every
precious
moment!
love!
B Biro

Brian D. Biro

Pygmalion Press books and tapes may be purchased for educational, business or sales promotional use. For information please call or write Pygmalion Press, 204 Weston Way, Asheville, NC 28803 or call (828) 654-8852.

Creative direction and design by The Terry Group, Virginia Beach, VA

Edited by Just Write

Dedication

To my wonderful sister, Katlin Hecox,
whose unselfish, compassionate,
and loyal spirit makes a shining difference
for everyone she touches.
Thank you Katlin for being so supportive,
caring, and FUN!
May you enjoy every precious moment!

Acknowledgements

I have been blessed with inestimable gifts from the wonderful coaches who have touched my life. Through their vision, insight, care, and wisdom, I began to see through the eyes of a coach. My heartfelt thanks to Tom Hansen, who taught me about real teamwork; Jim Andersen, who exemplified the positive Pygmalion spirit; my parents, Lou and Miriam Biro, who showed me how to live with energy and personal responsibility; Doug Hanson, who reminds me every day to keep my "Eager Meter" on full; Shore Slocum for his spiritual wisdom and mastery of moments; Nick Daley, Kate Rander, Larry Michel, and Raphiella Adamson for helping me understand what *unconditional* really means; Katlin Hecox for manifesting true servant leadership; Robert Mott, Karen Risch, and Terry Finder for their artistic brilliance and vitality; and Lou Tice, Stephen Covey, Jack Canfield, Mark Victor Hansen, Hyrum Smith, Bob Proctor, Daryl and Marta Kollman, the Robbins family (John, Deo, and Ocean), Jim Rohn, Monty Roberts, Morrie Schwarz, Joseph Girzone, John Wooden, Mahatma Gandhi, Mother Teresa, and Jesus for the inspiration they so freely shared and that fills my spirit in every precious moment.

Most of all, I thank my three greatest coaches: my wife, Carole, and my two children, Kelsey and Jenna. I feel like the luckiest man on the face of the earth because of the love and purpose they bring to my life.

Introduction

This book is written to open a whole new vision about coaching beyond the playing field. Ultimately every one of us is a coach. The people we affect as coaches include our children, our teammates and employees in our work, our friends, and the person we see in the mirror each day. Throughout this book I offer fresh, positive ideas about coaching in every area of life. Two areas particularly near and dear to our hearts — our family and our business — will receive special focus.

Coaching in the Family

No where in today's lightning fast, complex, and often confusing world is the need for a fresh perspective more imperative than in the family. We have been stunned and frightened by violence and murder committed by teenagers and even younger children. Fingers have been pointed in blame at the media, the entertainment industry, the NRA and gun advocates. But we do not need more blame, we need action and responsibility. The legendary Alabama football coach, Paul Bear Bryant once said, "I'm just an old country plowhand, but I've learned one thing if you want to get a team's heart beating as one. When things go great, THEY did it. When things go pretty good, WE did it. When things go bad, I did it!" Coach Bryant had it right, the only way we can become an example of responsibility, is to be responsible!

We CAN change this tragic trend among our youth by taking the responsibility to adopt the coaching perspective as parents and create fresh habits based upon the foundational principles that fill this book. As you begin to see through the eyes of a coach, you will become more and more clear about the actions you can take to build confidence, unselfishness, faith, and compassion in your children. You will discover the secrets that let your children know without question that they are important. You will find it far easier to instill self-discipline, raise your children's standards, and expand your connection and enjoyment every step along the path from infancy to adulthood. Ultimately by dedicating yourself to these simple principles you will build lifelong friendships with your children based upon honesty, openness, and mutual respect. Can you think of anything more deeply satisfying in life than creating this kind of loving relationship with your children? There is certainly no better platform upon which your children can build rich, joyful, and meaningful lives.

Some of the ideas in this book will require tenacity and dedication to change. You will need to break a deeply ingrained habit and become a "master asker" rather than a "typical teller." You will have to discipline yourself to live your highest priorities and be more fully present with your family members in your precious moments together. You will need to learn that the love you fail to share is the only pain you live with. The time to express your appreciation, love, and admiration is now because there is no guarantee you will have another chance. You will need to elevate your level of energy and live with greater vitality and alertness than ever before.

It sounds like a tall order! But you will find that as you fill with the vision of a coach you will get in touch with the most powerful source of inspiration, energy, and passion—your true purpose. Children are the most radiant gifts of all from God. As a parent there is nothing you wouldn't do to give your kids the very best opportunity to live magnificent lives. When you combine this sacred purpose with the insights and wisdom that come into focus through the eyes of a coach, you will be amazed at the transformation ignited in you, and through you to all you touch.

Coaching in Business

The most crucial and highly praised skill in the business world today is not an understanding of interest rates and stock values, or mastery of technology, the internet, or emerging markets. If you can't bring out the best in those around you and yourself, your future will become a dead-end. The name of the game from retail to high tech, from service industries to network marketing is coaching—building teams and inspiring confidence, unselfishness, infectious enthusiasm, and possibility thinking among those you lead and serve.

Coaching in business starts with an unusual, barrier-breaking attitude. You must see yourself as a <u>servant leader.</u> You recognize servant leaders the most when they are not there because it feels as if the glue has fallen out. They lead not by position or title, but rather by doing whatever it takes to elevate the team. As a top business coach today and into the future you must work *with* teammates and employees, you no longer see them as working *for* you. Your ultimate goal is to support each individual in rising to his or her highest level. You live each day with the basic credo that credit is something you give, responsibility something you take.

Business coaching excellence requires the same keen alertness as parenting when it comes to understanding and inspiring those around you. You do not strive to motivate and guide everyone in the same way because everyone is different. Some thrive on praise or a pat on the back. Others need to be challenged, while still others respond best by setting high standards and giving them space to perform. Only by paying close attention and having the flexibility to change your approach can you know the best way to coach each individual. It's a constantly challenging, stimulating, and energizing reward that makes coaching so exciting.

Probably the biggest challenge as you grow into a champion business coach is to move from ego to "we go." The great Olympic track champion, Wilma Rudolph beautifully expressed the simple awareness that makes this transformation in attitude possible when she said, "No matter what you accomplish, somebody helped you." We never break through alone. As a great coach, if you want respect, give it away. If you want loyalty, be intensely loyal. If you want energy, commitment, and unselfishness in your team, become a shining reflection of these qualities.

Throughout this book you will find dozens of ideas and principles to apply as a coach in your business. They will work as effectively in your work as in your family if you constantly replenish your genuine attitude of gratitude and will fail if your goal is to *get.* This winning attitude begins with simple appreciation to the Creator for giving you the tools, choices, and responsibility to impact others. Buoyed by this spiritual foundation of thanks, and strengthened by faith that there is always a way when you're committed, you'll find new enjoyment, constant purpose, and accelerating success in your career as you begin to see through the eyes of a coach.

Contents

What is my most important long-term role as a human being?

c h a p t e r   o n e

Your Secret Identity: Uncovering Your Surprising Inner Self

You are really quite remarkable. Every day you play so many roles and tackle so many challenges. Professional, friend, student, teammate, parent, chauffeur, cheerleader, disciplinarian, time planner, teacher, psychologist, motivational speaker, money manager, problem solver—the list goes on and on. When you stop to think about it, you realize you're even the CEO of your own life! And, whether you recognize it or not, you make a difference in the lives of others through your example, energy, thoughts, and actions.

With so many hats to wear and responsibilities to shoulder, it's easy to feel overwhelmed. There's so much to do and so little time! It's a rare treat to take a moment to consider key questions about your purpose, direction, and identity. Yet fundamental questions like these can change your life:

- What is my most important long-term role as a human being?
- How do I know where to best direct my focus in

the midst of so much activity?

- Is there an *identity* I can create for myself that can fill me with ongoing purpose, elevate my energy, and expand my happiness?

- Is there a common thread I can weave through the myriad things I *do* to help me understand who I really *am?*

We are at our best when we have a purpose that is bigger than ourselves. When Mother Teresa said, "Service is love in action," in just five powerful words, she helped us see that there is nothing that fulfills, frees, and fires us up more than seeking to make a difference in others' lives. It's one of the most inspiring truths about human beings: **People will often do more for others than they will do for themselves.**

We are at best when we have a purpose bigger than ourselves.

If we are to assume an identity that will allow us to live with character and reach our full potential, it *must* be one that involves service to others. And the greatest service we can provide is to help others bring out *their* full potential, to help them believe in themselves. That is why the pivotal role that will *inspire* us when we see it, *energize* us when we accept it, and *transform* us when we live it, is that of a *coach.*

Each of us has our own reaction and perception when we think of a coach. Perhaps you envision a chair-throwing drill master with an in-your-face, my-way-or-the-highway style. Or you may think of a wise, patient, and kindly individual who motivates not by fear, but rather by being your friend and mentor. For many, the word *coach* immediately conjures athletics, yet more and more the term becomes ingrained in business, financial planning, education, spiritual guidance, health, and family. As you read this book, you will discover that a coach is not so much a job description confined to a profession, but rather a way of seeing yourself holistically—an identity—that reaches into every area of your life.

When you see yourself as a coach, you see differently. You automatically make new choices. You change your actions. You grow nonstop because whenever you seek to enrich another person's experience, you can't help but enrich your own. There is a great coach already inside of you for your friends, your business associates, your children, and yourself.

When you see yourself as a coach, you see differently.

Though we most often think of coaching as a way of relating to others, we first and foremost coach *ourselves*. The results we generate as self-coaches will be revealed to others every day as our example, which in turn becomes the most influential instrument we use in bringing out their greatness.

You're about to explore principles and strategies vital to becoming a superb coach—whether you're working with others or trying to improve yourself. Some of these principles are surprising. They go against the grain of traditional ways of viewing leadership and coaching. Others may seem so simple that your first reaction may be, "I already know that!" But remember what the greatest college basketball coach in history, John Wooden, often said: "It's what you learn after you know everything that makes the difference." The closer you look at the strategies and principles, the more possibility you will discover within each.

To get started, it's imperative that you understand one foundational truth about coaching, or you may doubt yourself and give up before you even try the coaching perspective on for size: Because coaching is not so much about teaching others what you know as it is about helping them discover, believe in, and act upon what *they* know, you need not know more than those you lead to be an effective coach. You do not have to be as proficient, skilled, talented, intelligent, or experienced as those you seek to serve. As a great coach, you seek to instill in them *self-motivation* that burns and inspires whether or not you are present. You want your team to understand and connect with your vision, but, above all, you want them to become clear, energized, and determined about their *own* vision.

Coaching is about helping others discover, believe in, and act upon what they know.

When you stop and think about it, you'll notice most of the finest coaches from virtually every field are not the finest players or practitioners themselves. These quality coaches are, however, masters at helping those they coach bring out their true abilities and believe in their own possibilities.

So let's begin by bringing into focus perhaps the most surprising principle you'll discover through the eyes of a coach: *Ask more than tell.*

Your team can tackle any mountain when they are coached to be leaders who think for themselves and act out of personal responsibility.

chapter two

Ask More Than Tell to Take Your Team to the Top!

Great coaches are master askers! This may seem to go against the grain of our typical view of coaches as strong-minded dictators with all the answers. But here is a truly liberating truth: **The quality of our teams will be determined by the quality of the questions we ask one another.** Leaders and coaches who *ask* more than *tell* create leaders rather than followers.

When we ask questions, we spark thought and stimulate discovery. We help others think for themselves. Over time, those we coach develop far greater insight and understanding that allows their vision to expand. By asking more than telling, we also breathe faith into others' hearts, which helps them take responsibility for their decisions and actions.

This doesn't mean there aren't times to give answers. It simply means that as a coach you want to help others become self-starters who think for themselves. A simple strategy for getting started on the path toward becoming a master asker is to discipline yourself to respond first with a question when people come to you for advice and answers. Instead of stepping forward right away to tackle their problems for them, first ask, "What do *you* think would be the best way to handle this?" Instantly you've let them know you truly value their ideas, and you've given them the chance to help themselves. Though initially they may feel somewhat uncomfortable or even disappointed that you didn't give them an answer, over time, the growing sense of personal responsibility you will foster with this strategy will help them strengthen their spirits, solution-orientation, and confidence.

When you ask for a response from someone, it is critical that you *really* listen. The secret is to listen for *their* answers, not yours. How many times do we ask questions trying to squeeze out the answer we want? By opening yourself to really listen, you have a much greater chance to learn. When you ask others for their ideas, be eager to hear approaches and viewpoints that had never occurred to you before. And welcome those fresh perspectives with genuine enthusiasm, because they have the greatest potential to create positive change in *your* life.

Leaders and coaches who ask more than tell create leaders rather than followers.

I received a real wake-up call about the power of asking more than telling when I took an honest look at my effectiveness as a coach of coaches.

Following my graduation from Stanford University, I had become a United States Swimming coach and built a small novice team into one of the largest privately owned swimming programs in the country. Our swimmers had achieved all kinds of outstanding results, finishing in the top three at the Junior Nationals, top ten at the Senior Nationals, with several of our kids qualifying for the Olympic trials. Probably most exciting, over forty of the young people I'd had the honor to coach earned college scholarships.

When I left coaching to pursue my master's degree, I felt great satisfaction about the accomplishments we had earned during the eight years of my tenure. But then I asked myself a question that really shook me up: *If I had been such a good coach, what happened to my assistant coaches when I left?* Ouch! Sometimes the truth can leave some major teethmarks on your ego!

You see, more than a year after I left coaching, most of my assistant coaches were floundering. All of them were talented, bright, and caring people. Yet when I had moved on, they'd gotten stuck. They hadn't quite known what to do. That is, except for one of my assistants who had continued to grow and improve and was flourishing in his chosen field of education. And, incidentally, when he'd first come to work for me, he'd been the least likely candidate to be a good swimming coach! He'd known virtually nothing about competitive swimming. He had been a baseball player who had never been on a swim team in his life.

When we ask questions, we spark thought and stimulate discovery.

Why did this one individual excel while all the others struggled? The more I thought about this question, the clearer the answer became. Jay was the one coach I had asked more than told!

With the other assistants, I had called all the shots. I'd told them exactly what to do and in what order. I'd treated them more like coaching robots than thinking, developing human beings. I hadn't even allowed them to make mistakes because I'd cover for them. I'd never asked them about strategies or their ideas on how to deal with challenges. As a result, I'd never given them the chance to think creatively or to grow into their potential.

But with Jay I had been a different kind of coach. Though he'd known little about swimming technique originally, his special gift for making the sport fun for children had been apparent from the beginning. The kids always loved him and couldn't wait to come to swim practice. This had filled me with great faith in Jay, and I'd found it increasingly natural to ask instead of tell. If he came to me with a question about how to handle a particular situation, I wouldn't answer. Instead I'd ask, "What do you think would work best?" I'd held strategy sessions with him where I'd ask for his ideas about how best to develop the team. I'd also asked Jay in more subtle yet equally empowering ways by not showing up at the meets and practices at which he was coaching. By giving him the ball without looking over his shoulder, I'd let him know that my belief in him was strong. When I left, he didn't miss a beat.

Asking is a win-win game!

Jay would have been the first to tell you that when he started coaching, he was a Kellogg's corn flake! But the power of asking more than telling is transformative. Today he is one of the most outstanding professionals in his field. He is a mentor teacher who coaches other teachers in working with disabled children.

What's more, by asking more than telling, I had gained every bit as much as Jay. I learned ideas, perspectives, and skills from him I use every single day as a father and a speaker that make immeasurable differences for those I love. Asking is a win-win game!

Following my graduation from Stanford University, I had become a United States Swimming coach and built a small novice team into one of the largest privately owned swimming programs in the country.

*When you require your team to accomplish a project **and have tons of fun in the process,** they are <u>required</u> to think differently about their strategy and approach.*

chapter   three

Turning "Have to" into "Love to!"

In my seminars and workshops, I often have participants play a hilarious and eye-opening game called
"Bottoms Up." As I set the stage for the game, I demonstrate a strategy for playing it then explain the goal of the
game very clearly and succinctly. It's a very simple game
wherein you and a partner must attempt to get your bottoms up—in fact, every part of your bodies off the ground
except your four hands—for the count of three. As soon
as the demonstration and instruction is complete, participants are invited to play the game. *Boom!* The room fills
with laughter and spirit—and a fair amount of confusion!
It looks like a crazy game of Twister® as participants
attempt all kinds of gymnastic maneuvers to successfully
achieve their goal.

After a couple of minutes of letting everyone struggle
with the challenge, I offer a simple clue. I stop them for a
moment and say, "If it's not working, try something
different." This is where the game really gets fun because
most participants look at me for a moment, think about
the clue—and then do exactly the same thing they had

been struggling with before I offered the hint! In most classes, less than ten percent even attempt something different, though it's clear to them that what they'd been doing was absolutely not working!

Perhaps the most telling part of the game is that this magnetic pull toward continually repeating the same ineffective strategy to achieve Bottoms Up comes from my one fifteen-second demonstration. As I explained the game, my words were straightforward and clear. But the impact of *my example delivered through my body language* was so strong that most participants became completely stuck in this one way of approaching the problem.

If it's not working, try something different– by asking yourself a new empowering question.

What are you doing in your life right now that feels like a force job? Are certain important tasks and responsibilities so distasteful that you continually put them off, even though you know it's critical that they be completed? What duties are so uncomfortable for you that the instant they come to mind you tighten up with feelings of frustration ("I can't do this!"), ineptitude ("I'm terrible at this!"), or indignation ("Why do I have to do this?")? The next time you encounter one of these obstacles, it's the perfect opportunity to apply the simple principle—if it's not working, try something different—by asking yourself a new, empowering question. Immediately you'll feel fresh energy and a sense of possibility.

Here are three questions that will completely transform the way you feel as you approach areas of challenge that previously left you squirming like a fish out of water or hustling to find some excuse to procrastinate.

1. How can I accomplish this task, project, or challenge and have tons of fun in the process? This question begins with the presumption that you *can* achieve your desired result. By adding the requirement that you must have tons of fun in the process, you will need to *think differently*, tapping into a part of your consciousness already primed with positive anticipation and sense of humor.

Ask yourself a simple question: "What's great about this?"

2. What's great about doing this task? This question helps you look for the sometimes hidden value you will receive from taking action. Legendary positive thinker Napoleon Hill wrote in *Think and Grow Rich*, "Every adversity, every failure, and every heartache carries with it the Seed of an equivalent or a greater Benefit." We nurture that seed by focusing on the benefits even when they initially appear to be outweighed by the adversity or our fears. Compelling whys often lead to breakthrough hows. For example, when I first began appearing on radio shows to promote my books, I was nervous and uneasy. Then I remembered to ask myself a simple question: "What's great about this?" In an instant, I realized that by enthusiastically participating on these shows, I would be able to rapidly reach thousands of people with ideas and

principles that can help them live happier, more meaningful lives. What's more, I could speak to them in their
cars and homes all over the country without having to
leave my family! I started smiling when I realized I could
connect with listeners while dressed in my running shorts
and T-shirt in the comfort of my home office. Suddenly I
felt excited and grateful rather than anxious. With my
new spirit, my performance improved dramatically, and I
created momentum where there had previously been hesitation. I participated in over two hundred radio inter-
views in less than a year!

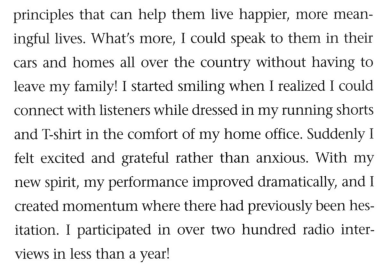

People will do far more for and with others than they will do for themselves.

**3. With whom can I team to achieve our
desired outcome?** Remember, people will do far more
for and with others than they will do for themselves.
When tackling a challenge you previously viewed as a
chore, joining with one or more other people with whom
you enjoy working opens fresh possibilities and generates
energy. Working as a team, you can merge strengths and
different talents that will save time while skyrocketing
your own motivation.

Once you've practiced asking *yourself* these questions
as you encounter obstacles and challenges, you'll find
they work equally well when you ask others. Simply
change from first to second person *(me to you, my to your,
etc.)*, and you are ready to ask questions that will help your
children, spouse, friends, and teammates help themselves!

Tuck your children in bed with a story and the three powerful Integration Questions:
   1. *What did you do today that you felt great about?*
   2. *What did you give today that made a difference for someone else?*
   3. *What are you looking forward to tomorrow?*

chapter four

InteGREAT Your Life by Getting Off the Roller Coaster

Every day we are bombarded with reminders that our lives are moving a whole lot faster. Projects we were once expected to complete in three days now must be finished in one. And wait until next week! Through technology we are seeing a staggering acceleration in the accumulation of data and knowledge. For example, more computer information is stored in a Buick Skylark today than in the Apollo Spacecraft that went to the moon in 1969! Five years from now we will be absolutely stunned at how primitive the cutting edge of today will have become.

In the midst of this extraordinary acceleration, one of the most important strategies to build into your life is to slow down on a regular basis to *integrate* what you've been experiencing. The process of integration is another powerful application of the "ask instead of tell" principle. We integrate by asking two foundational questions: "What have we learned?" and "How will we apply what we've learned?"

When we integrate, we add value and insight to our previous efforts, actions, and strategies. We also decrease the likelihood that we will repeat mistakes and errors in judgment. We get off the roller coaster of frustration that comes when we try harder and harder rather than adjusting and changing. When we integrate, we use rather than waste the gift of feedback. Perhaps most important, by reinforcing lessons, principles, and insights that serve us, we sharply boost the accessibility of this valuable information. Every experience and perception we have is recorded in the unmatched computer system known as the human mind. Integrating speeds up the computer, enabling us to more readily retrieve the information we need, when we need it. Integrating is also great fun! It brings meaning and understanding to our efforts, successes, and even disappointments.

Slow down on a regular basis to integrate what you've been experiencing.

There are three primary ways to integrate. **First is to integrate with a buddy who is a part of your team and has been involved in similar experiences and challenges.** This one-on-one integration is both comfortable and energizing. Almost everyone is at ease talking with a buddy who has been in similar circumstances we have faced. As a result, the insights and ideas that are sparked by asking the integration questions flow easily in a one-on-one exchange. What's more, the buddies motivate one another, creating synergy that expands each individual's awareness and clarity. As your buddy answers the integration questions, you'll flash upon ideas that needed only the spark of his or her thought to solidify into a fresh "Aha!"

When working in teams, a second valuable way to integrate is to hold a session where you

pose the integration questions to the whole group. The biggest benefit of whole-group integration is that each idea or "synergy spark" reaches the entire team versus just one other teammate. The challenge, however, is that in most teams there are some individuals who simply won't speak up in a big group. Thus, their involvement and contributions are stymied. They become observers rather than active participants. That's why it's better to use full-group integration as a supplement to one-on-one conversation, but not as the sole method. Both of these interactive ways of integrating are important tools for you as a coach. By facilitating the process of integration with your teams, you will invite progress, inspire personal responsibility, and instill a constantly renewing commitment to growth. In the long run, integrating will help your team replace the often paralyzing fear of failure with an activating love of learning.

When we integrate, we use rather than waste the gift of feedback.

A third way to integrate is to ask *yourself* the integrating questions and record your thoughts in a journal, computer, or tape recorder. This internal integration is richly fulfilling because you crystallize thoughts that would otherwise swirl around unorganized and inaccessible in your subconscious. As you record your thoughts, you feel the inner satisfaction of increased understanding and take a giant step toward improved actions.

When you look through the eyes of a coach, you'll begin to see that the last impression left today becomes the starting point of tomorrow. That's why integrating builds momentum within your team by ending every practice, meeting, or day on an up note. This is especially important because of the way most people hold onto disappointments, rejections, and failures in total disproportion to life's small wins and achievements.

Because what we focus on is what we create, I encourage you to use a simple but effective strategy to help those around you end each day on a positive note. In addition to the integrating questions about what you've learned today and how you will apply what you've learned, three other questions will ignite positive anticipation about tomorrow by focusing on the blessings of today. As you close a meeting, complete a day at the office, or tuck your children in for the night, ask these three powerful integrating questions:

What we focus on is what we create!

- **What did you do today that you felt great about?**

- **What did you give today that made a difference for someone else?**

- **What are you looking forward to tomorrow?**

As we ask these integrating questions we enhance others' belief in possibility and opportunity. Most of all, we support their faith in themselves, the central vision to keep in focus through the eyes of a coach.

The difference between a good team and a great team lies in the difference between "willing to support" and "eager to do whatever it takes."

chapter five

Build Unstoppable Enthusiasm With the "Eager Meter"

I once asked John Wooden, arguably the greatest coach in history, a question that cut right to the core of what's most important in building championship teams: What's the difference between a good team and a great one? I expected Coach Wooden to respond first by emphasizing the importance of recruiting. In other words, you have to recruit the most talented people if you are going to rise to the top. But Coach Wooden surprised me when he said, "Recruiting is important, but definitely not most important. **After forty years as a teacher, coach, and parent I believe the pivotal difference centers around two words—*willing* and *eager*.** On good or average teams, everyone associated with the team is *willing* to support each other. Willing means, yes, I'll do it, but I don't really want to. It's the same kind of feeling you get when you ask your children to clean their rooms. Yes, I'll do it because I want to *eat*—but I don't really want to! On championship teams, those that get the most from who they are, everyone associated with the team is *eager* to do whatever it takes to support one another and the goals of the team as a whole. No job is too big or too small."

Coach Wooden's answer to my question immediately conjured an image in my mind I now call "the Eager Meter."

Check Your E-Meter 3 Times Daily
Give yourself an honest rating
of your "E"nergy level:

1 = " I can't get off the couch."
5 = " I can move, but my energy's kinda low."
10 = " I'm so pumped, I could jump-start your car!"

THIS WEEK	Morning Reading	Midday Reading	Evening Reading
DAY 1			
DAY 2			
DAY 3			
DAY 4			
DAY 5			
DAY 6			
DAY 7			

NEXT MONTH	Morning Reading	Midday Reading	Evening Reading
DAY 1			
DAY 2			
DAY 3			
DAY 4			
DAY 5			
DAY 6			
DAY 7			

As a coach, teacher, leader, or parent, nothing is more important to those you serve in the long run than the degree to which you inspire movement on the meter toward eagerness, because it requires energy, unselfishness, commitment, humor, and spirit.

The first step in helping others elevate their Eager Meters is to elevate your own. One remarkably potent strategy to make a shift is to notice for one full week the number of times you catch yourself saying or thinking that you have to do something. The key words are have to. Every time you notice have to coming out of your mouth or in your self-talk, replace the words with *want to, choose to, like to,* or *love to.*

The first step in helping others elevate their Eager Meter is to elevate your own.

When you think about it, in life there is only one thing you have to do, and that is to die—everything else is a matter of choice. Yet we learned to say "I have to" when we were children. The words were ingrained in our subconscious along with two other words that triggered action. Those two words were, *or else.* We were told, "You have to do x, y, and z—or else something very bad is going to happen!" Though the "or else" threat was often effective in getting us to take action, it was fear-based. It made us feel controlled instead of in charge of our lives. As we grew older the "or else" slid into the subconscious but was never lost. That feeling of panic, overwhelm, and anxiety that comes whenever we feel we have to do something never fails to increase stress.

As you begin to say, "I want to," "I choose to," "I like to," or "I love to" even for routine types of tasks, you will spark a dynamic shift in your Eager Meter. You will rediscover that you really do have choices and that with personal responsibility comes joy, peace of mind, and optimism.

You'll enjoy abundant enthusiasm when you're truly living your purpose.

c h a p t e r   s i x

Have a "Purpose Party" to Skyrocket Self-Motivation

Sometimes your most important job as a coach is to ensure that your team and each of its individuals keeps their purpose fresh and alive. The biggest challenge to maintaining this focus is fear. Sometimes the fear will show up as avoidance: Rather than giving full effort with enthusiasm, your teammates will slip into procrastination, uninspired routine, or even resentment. At other times you may notice fear rearing its ugly head as stress, ill temper, and frustration. You'll see good people tighten up rather than lighten up. Their fear is infecting them with subconscious thoughts of *I can't do it,* or *I'll never be able to get this done,* or even *What if I don't measure up?*

How can you counteract these fears? Ever heard of a "pity party"? Forget it! One of the best strategies to renew your teammates' courage and enthusiasm is to have a "purpose party." When you notice signs of fear popping up among your teammates, children, or friends, it's a prime opportunity to refresh their sense of purpose so they can replace fear with possibility. In a comfortable atmosphere away from the heat of battle for a while, ask them questions that will help them rekindle excitement and vitality about their purpose. Simply ask, **"What is your desired outcome?"** and follow with, **"What will it mean to you when you've achieved it?"** When you add a third question—**"What will it mean to the people you care about for you to reach your desired outcome?"**—once again you tap into the heightened inspiration that comes from being part of a team. Remember, most people will do more for others than they will do for themselves. Your goal as the coach is to evoke positive emotion about why their efforts have meaning, value, and importance. When people feel their work serves an important purpose, they are self-motivated, proactive, and happy.

Your goal as the coach is to evoke positive emotion about why their efforts have meaning, value and importance.

Have some fun with this strategy. Once you've helped your teammates center on their purpose by asking the questions, you can add energy and spirit by using some creativity. Supply everyone with poster boards, markers, magazines for cutting out pictures, scissors, and paste. Let them have a blast making their own "purpose poster" that will become a visual reminder of how valuable and worthwhile their desired outcome really is. When the posters are finished, invite each individual to put theirs up where they will see it everyday. Another way you can bring this strategy to life is to have your teammates buddy-up and ask one another the questions in an "interview session." I've used this process dozens of times with a variety of teams and always had terrific results. You'll see energy and connection grow right before your eyes!

Wow!! I really can see myself differently!

chapter seven

The Secret of New Vision: How to Change Your Lenses to Discover New Possibilities

Look at the sentence written below.

FINISHED FILES ARE THE RESULT OF YEARS

OF SCIENTIFIC

STUDY COMBINED WITH THE EXPERIENCE

OF MANY

YEARS OF

EXPERTS.

It probably doesn't make a whole lot of sense to you now, but within this sentence is a secret that can change your life! Please take a moment now to read the sentence once more, but this time for the fun of it, count the times you see the letter F. Read it through just one more time, counting your Fs as you go. Did you find two Fs? Three Fs? Four, five, or even more Fs?

Now it gets fun! Go back to the sentence and as you read it through once again, look for the word "of", and then count your Fs! Wow! Did a whole bunch more of those pesky Fs suddenly appear? I'll bet you now have found seven Fs. Isn't that a kick?

I have an important question for you now. Why didn't

you see the Fs in the first place? Incidentally, when I first played this game I was so sure I had three Fs on my card that I argued with the workshop instructor! I said, "I don't know about you, buddy, but I have three Fs!" When I found out there were more I thought to myself, "What else am I missing that's right in front of my eyes?"

There is an important reason most of us miss the Fs. The secret is that the F in the word *of* doesn't sound like an F. Think back to long ago, when you learned to read. You probably learned to read phonetically, by sounding words out. So, when you learned the word *of* it was actually *uv*. Once you learned to see of as if it was uv, the next step in the learning process was to repeat it over and over until you had it down pat. In other words, you had to condition this way of seeing the word *of* until it was natural and automatic.

We might be missing something about who we are because of the way we've been conditioned to see ourselves.

This process of conditioning, by first learning to see or perceive in a certain way, and then repeating that vision, action, or process over and over until it is ingrained, is the way we learn most things. For example, we're not born knowing what a chair is. We have to associate the word *chair* with the actual object upon which we sit until the word has meaning. Isn't that the same way we learn to do our jobs, work with people, and face challenges? In fact, isn't that the same way we learn who we are?

So here's the big question. Since the reason we don't see the Fs in the word *of* is that we were conditioned not to, is it possible we might be missing something about who we are because of the way we've been conditioned to see ourselves? Or not to see ourselves? There are Fs far more important than letters in a game. There are Fs that can help us become more loving parents, more effective professionals, better leaders, and that can help us find more possibility, solutions, fun, and love in every precious moment.

The secret is to change our "lenses."

How did I help you find all the Fs? First, remember what I *didn't* do. I didn't ask you to look *harder*. (If you were like me the first time I played the game, you were trying your best and still could find only some of the Fs.) Instead, I simply asked you to look for *something different*. As soon as you adjusted your lenses and looked for the word *of* instead of the Fs, they jumped out at you so clearly, you had to laugh that you had missed them in the first place!

Try adjusting your lenses to look for qualities and possibilities you didn't initially see.

But, we're not done yet. Here's the best part: We still haven't found all the Fs! Can you adjust your lenses again? By breaking the conditioning of looking for the F sounds and discovering the *ofs*, you now have found seven Fs. But as you look once more at the sentence, look not for the words or letters, but rather for the graphic pattern the sentence makes. You've got it—another F!

In becoming a human being of great compassion, understanding, creativity, and inspiration, a wonderfully worthwhile goal is to become a "World-Class F-Finder"! Whenever you find yourself with the person you're pretty certain God put on the planet to bug you, try adjusting your lenses to look for qualities and possibilities you didn't initially see. When you find yourself stuck on a problem or challenge that is beginning to frustrate you, try reversing your assumptions and see what you come up with. When you look in the mirror and see only your faults or fears, look again. There is more in you—more beauty, more heart, more strength, and more love than you've been seeing with your old lenses. And most of all, remember that it is the Fs you haven't seen yet that will change your life!

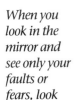

When you look in the mirror and see only your faults or fears, look again.

My wife and I use the Just Listen strategy with wonderful results. It's our way to routinely "check in" and see how we're feeling.

c h a p t e r   e i g h t

Turn Down the Heat: "Just Listening" to Diffuse Anger

Your daughter screams at you in exasperation, "You're ruining my life!" as she runs from the room. Your crime? You've just told her that the speech she is supposed to deliver in school tomorrow isn't long enough to meet the two-minute minimum requirement—somehow she must come up with at least thirty more seconds of information. No, she cannot stretch the presentation out by speaking in ultra-slow motion. There's no way around it; she is going to have to get back to work. She can't play on the Internet, or call her friend and gab away, until after the job is done and done well. She looks at you in complete horror. How could you be such a cruel parent?

It all sounds so silly when you step back from the heat of the moment and look at the facts. Yet how often do we overreact to overreactions? When exasperation and frustration are met by defensiveness, sound-proof walls are immediately erected and any possibility of real listening vanishes. **Anger does not diminish anger—only love does.** As a coach it's critical to remember that if you try to make lasting, positive impact in the heat of the moment, you're going to get burned! Shut off the burner for a while and get back together when things have cooled down. When you implement this simple strategy you'll be amazed at the progress you'll make.

One of the best ways to turn off the heat is to hold occasional "just listen" sessions with important people in your life. As its name implies, a just-listen session gives others a chance to be fully heard. Your job is to just listen once you've set the stage by explaining what the session is all about.

A just-listen session brings perspective and understanding back into focus.

My wife and I have used this strategy with wonderful results for many years. In the midst of the whirlwind we call family life, we can easily become so caught up in the busy-ness of what we're doing that we forget to check in with each other so we can see how we're *feeling*. Without making time to truly listen to one another, those little life irritants like not closing the toilet seat and forgetting to put the cap back on the toothpaste can begin to multiply. Remarks made in a rushed moment can linger and begin to fester in the subconscious, away from reason and context. The next thing you know you're upset with one another and don't really know why.

A just-listen session brings perspective and understanding back into focus. It's a simple process wherein you make time to get together for fifteen minutes to a half-hour of uninterrupted attention. When you meet, each of you pledges to listen to the other for five to fifteen minutes straight—without saying one single word! No matter what is said to you, you just listen.

The benefits of these sessions are enormous. First of all, you learn within about ninety seconds that when you let go of formulating your response while someone else is speaking, you easily slip into his or her shoes. You become truly present with your partner where she is in that moment. You feel her feelings and see through her eyes. Even if you disagree with what is being said, you completely understand how those thoughts were generated. Defensiveness evaporates and compassion escalates. For one thing, you can't possibly remember all that is being said!

If you listen, you let go of formulating your response while someone else is speaking. Then, you can easily slip into his or her shoes.

As each of you get to speak your piece, not only do you "feel heard," but you also see your partner fully listening. This creates a tremendous feeling of connection and desire to reciprocate. Suddenly you *want* to listen to each other.

When I was the vice-president of a large training company I used a just-listen session to break through a potentially destructive situation with Raphiella, the head of our customer service department. She was intensely loyal to the man I had replaced as vice-president and harbored strong feelings of anger and blame toward me. No matter how I tried to set our relationship on a positive track, nothing worked. The iciness between us was evident to everyone in our department and was a huge obstacle blocking any kind of forward momentum.

I asked Raphiella if she would agree to get together with me for just twenty minutes. I made every effort to set a time that would be convenient for her and did my best to create an environment that was quiet and calm, away from the heat of battle. She agreed reluctantly to meet with me.

When she arrived, I thanked her sincerely for taking the time to try to improve our working relationship. I told her how important it was for us to find a way to work well together and praised her for the superb job she did for our customers every day. I also told her the truth about our rift, without embellishment or anger. There was no question that we had failed to build a good relationship up until now and I couldn't think of anything that was more crucial to the future of our team than improving our connection.

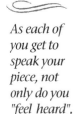

As each of you get to speak your piece, not only do you "feel heard", but you also see your partner fully listening.

Then I explained the just-listen process. I asked her if she would talk to me for ten minutes about whatever she felt important. My promise was that no matter what she said, I would just listen. After her ten minutes, it would be my turn and she would become the listener. She said, "I don't think I can talk for ten minutes."

I replied, "Would you try?"

One hour later she stopped talking! In that hour I kept my promise faithfully. I didn't say a word. I learned so much about this terrific person and what had been eating at her spirit. For the first time it became obvious to me why Raphiella was so admired by those she served. She had unstoppable passion for taking care of her customers and teammates. I had never seen these qualities so clearly because I had always been too busy dodging her bullets or trying mightily to be patient.

Even more remarkable were the changes in her perspective. In that hour of simple communication and listening, she talked herself into a lifelong friendship with me. She saw that her anger and unhappiness was not really about me. I just happened to be the one who took over for someone she felt had been unfairly treated. The more she talked, the more she opened to my enthusiasm, energy, and desire to create success for everyone associated with our team. By listening and arranging a peaceful environment away from the heat of battle, I was able to build more loyalty and teamwork than I could have possibly hoped for. After that just-listen session our entire organization began to fly!

Coaching excellence is not only a matter of what you say and do. It's also a matter of *when!* The time to build a bridge is not in the middle of a storm. It's much easier to get two hearts beating as one when you slow down the beat.

A just listen session creates a tremendous feeling of connection and desire to reciprocate.

Coaching is not so much about trying to cram more into those you guide, but rather about illuminating the big things that make the biggest difference in what kind of human beings they become.

chapter nine

Inspiring Others (and Yourself) With the Big Picture

Have you ever noticed that in virtually every team of people there are those who keep the parking brake locked tight until they have a solid idea of where they are going? I call these "big picture people." When they know their destination and direction, big picture people often become your most energized and enthusiastic team players. But, when left in the dark about the overall purpose and goals, they are easily frustrated and pessimistic. That's why one of the simple but often overlooked secrets to coaching and inspiring others is to communicate the big picture early, consistently, and clearly.

In the "F-card" game we played earlier, the eighth F represents the big picture, hidden from view until we step away and look from a different perspective. The human being can hold only one visual image in mind at a time. As a coach, it's crucial to train yourself to look at both the big picture and the details. Since you can see only one of those perspectives at a time, you must become a master of the LO-LO principle, which stands for lock-on/lock-off. This principle explains why it is necessary to "lock-off" from the details from time to time if you want to see the whole more clearly, and vice versa. Looking at the big picture helps you develop patience. You realize that long-term growth often requires many short-term adjustments. With the big picture in focus, it is easier to remember your real priorities and to lighten up and let go, rather than to smother.

For example, in the specialized coaching role known as parenting, it is easy to become so embroiled in day-to-day schedules and problems that we lose sight of our ultimate goals for our children. If you're a parent like me, your number one goal for your children is for them to *believe in themselves*, to know they have the ability, energy, and courage to overcome adversity and live fully. Yet, for me, in the face of my children's occasionally messy rooms and defiant tones, along with all the other bumps in the road to growing up, I can forget to keep the big picture in sight. I can get lost in the little things, which in the long run don't mean much.

Without the big-picture perspective, it's like trying to find someone's home without an address or phone number.

Without the big-picture perspective, it's like trying to find someone's home without an address or phone number. Even a map and compass are useless without knowing your destination. **But as soon as you step back and focus on the big picture, you easily make new choices, discover the peace that comes with greater patience, and formulate creative, effective strategies to move in the right direction.**

A while back, I was reading about an expert on the subject of time management who, when speaking to a group of business students, used an illustration they'd never forget. His wonderful short story serves as a refreshing reminder about keeping the big picture in sight.

As this man stood in front of the group of high-powered overachievers, he said, "Okay, time for a quiz."

He pulled out a one-gallon, wide-mouthed mason jar and set it on a table in front of him. Then he produced about a dozen fist-sized rocks and carefully placed them, one at a time, into the jar.

When the jar was filled to the top and no more rocks would fit inside, he asked, "Is this jar full?"

Everyone in the class said yes.

If you don't put the "big rocks" in first, you'll never get them in at all.

"Really?" he replied. He reached under the table and pulled out a bucket of gravel and poured some into the jar. When he shook it, pieces of gravel worked themselves down into the spaces between the big rocks.

He asked the group once more, "Is the jar full?"

By this time the class was onto him. "Probably not," one of them answered.

"Good!" the expert replied. This time he brought out a bucket of sand to pour into the jar. Once it had filled all the spaces left between the rocks and the gravel, he again asked the question: "Is this jar full?"

"No!" the class shouted. Once again he said, "Good!" Then he picked up a pitcher of water and poured it in until the jar was filled to the brim. Then he looked up at the class and asked, "What is the point of this illustration?"

One eager fellow raised his hand and said, "The point is that no matter how full your schedule is, if you try really hard, you can always fit some more things into it!"

"No," the speaker replied, "that's not the point. The truth this illustration teaches us is this: If you don't put the big rocks in first, you'll never get them in at all."

What are the "big rocks" in your life? A project you want to accomplish? Time with loved ones? Your faith? Your education? Your finances? A cause? Teaching or coaching others? Adventuring? Remember to put these big rocks in first, or you'll never get them in at all.

What are the "big rocks" in your life?

Coaching is not so much about trying to cram more into those you guide, but rather about illuminating the big things that make the biggest difference in what kind of human beings they become. By helping others remember the big picture and to fill their jars first with the "big rocks"—their most important priorities and goals—you will energize and motivate as never before. You'll assist those around you to replace stress with balance and anxiety with enthusiasm.

Simply by being more present you will be amazed at the transformation in all your relationships, personal and professional.

chapter ten

The Truly Precious Present: How Focus Builds Extraordinary Relationships

If there is one, most important thing you can do that will make you a better coach and help you live a rich and fulfilling life, it is to become fully present with all you touch. This will make the biggest difference for you as a parent, friend, teammate, teacher, business person, student, or any other role you may play in life. Being fully present means one hundred percent of your mind, body, and spirit are truly *there* with the people who are with you, focused on them in that moment. That may not seem like such a big deal at first, but sometimes the best way to clearly see the impact of a principle is to take an honest look at its opposite.

I'm not proud of it, but I have been a classic example of not being present with those I love most deeply at important times in our lives. Several years ago, when I was the vice-president of a major training company, I was totally swept up in my own career. I was so focused on my work that I left my home for the office every morning at 4:40 A.M. I just *had* to be the first one there. Each night I'd arrive home around 6 P.M. and found myself on the road teaching seminars or visiting our various franchise locations on many weekends. It wasn't at all uncommon for me to stay at the office much later on many weekday evenings, as well.

That was the year my oldest daughter, Kelsey, had just turned five. It was her first year in kindergarten, one of those milestones that arrive with such anticipation but seem to pass in an instant.

Being fully present means one hundred percent of your mind, body, and spirit are truly there with the people who are with you.

Though our whole family was excited about Kelsey's beginning steps in school, I was so driven in my work, not once did I see her wake up and get ready for her day. Not once was I there to make her breakfast or to drive her to kindergarten. Not once did I show up after school unexpectedly for a "dad and me" surprise. I thought about being there a hundred times but always managed to put it off. I rationalized that I'd make it up to her sometime soon.

Yet every night, when I walked in the house at six o'clock, I was met with the same miracle. My beautiful daughter stopped whatever she was doing as soon as she heard the door open, sprinted to me as fast as she could run, and literally leaped into my arms. As she hugged me with all her might, she looked up at me with her shining brown eyes and said, "Daddy, I love you so much! And Daddy, I *missed* you so much today!" Then she would gush with excitement as she told me about all the things that had happened to her all day. (And, if you remember, when you're five years old, cool things happen!)

And I missed it.

I didn't hear a word she said.

You see, when I walked into the house, the only part of me that showed up was my body. My mind, heart, and spirit were back at the office or worrying about what I had to do tomorrow. I was *never* present.

This went on for days that ran into weeks that rolled into months. Then one morning as I drove to work before 5 A.M., it was as if God had decided enough was enough and smacked me in the gut with an invisible sledgehammer. I felt an intense tightening in my stomach, and the next thing I knew, tears began to well up in my eyes, and I began to sob. I pulled to the side of the road filled with the vision of Kelsey and the truth.

To live a rich and fulfilling life it is important to become fully present with all you touch.

The truth was that she wasn't running to me any more. And even if I managed to wake up enough before she went to sleep at night to ask her, "What happened in your day?" her answer had become completely predictable: "Nothing," or "I don't know." At one time, she couldn't wait to tell me everything. Now it took a crowbar to pry any information from her. *Nothing* and *I don't know* come from *not* being present.

Through my tears that morning I saw for the first time what we communicate to others when we are fully present. **Our presence sends the unmistakable message: "You are important!"** And not being present sends an equally powerful message—one that my precious daughter was receiving loud and clear. My lack of presence cried out to Kelsey that she must not mean as much to daddy as all the "stuff" he does all day and thinks about all the time.

That morning, humbled by the realization of my self-ishness, and determined to become the kind of father Kelsey deserved, I changed the foremost goal in my life. It's a simple goal, yet one I had never heard before. My number one goal as a father, husband, coach, speaker, writer, and human being is to be *fully present* as much as I possibly can. I realized that morning for the first time that the only way I will ever touch another person's life is by being fully present with them.

Being present is not a technique. It is a choice that will enrich your life like no other.

Soon after that pivotal morning, I made some major changes in my life. I decided I would not wait until my children were grown and gone to understand how impor-tant our time is together. I would stop taking my wife and all she brings to our lives every day for granted. Today, I am most often the one who wakes my children up, cooks their breakfasts, makes their lunches, and drives them to school. I limit the number of speaking engagements I will accept each month so that I live my word about being fully present for my family. My life has never been so abundant.

Do you know the best part about being present? You can't fake it! How long does it take you to know when someone is not fully present? Can you tell over the phone? Being present is not a technique. It is a choice that will enrich your life like no other. And it is a decision you can make today.

Inch by inch, anything's a cinch! For the next thirty days, why don't you pick out one person in your life with whom you commit to be more present? That doesn't mean you have to spend more time with the person you've chosen. You may not have that luxury. It simply means that when you are together, you set aside the newspaper, shut off the television, and really listen. Look at that special person with fresh eyes and an open heart. There's a good chance you'll discover some new "Fs"! Once you've experienced the deepened connection you've built from this first concentrated effort at being present, you'll be hungry for more.

Simply by being more present you will be amazed at the transformation in your relationships, at the energy and spontaneity that flows naturally into your life, and at the expansion of love and joy that elevates your spirit in every precious moment!

No single choice will make a bigger difference in the kind of coach you become than being fully present. You will build confidence, loyalty, and commitment in everyone you touch.

No single choice will make a bigger difference in the kind of coach you become than being fully present.

The past is history
The future a mystery
The gift is *now*
That's why we call it the *present!*

*My grandmother, Ruby, was a dazzling beauty at nineteen and even
more beautiful when she opened her heart to me many, many years later.*

c h a p t e r   e l e v e n

Wednesdays With Ruby

The rewards that come from being present may not always be immediately apparent, but the impact on your life and everyone around you will be enormous in the long run. Recently I read a deeply moving book entitled *Tuesdays With Morrie: An Old Man, A Young Man, and the Last Great Lesson* (Doubleday, 1997) authored by a well-known sports columnist, Mitch Albom. This is a book that digs into the essence of what being fully present can mean to you and those you love.

The true story centers on Albom's Tuesday visits with his mentor and life coach, professor Morrie Schwartz, who was dying from Lou Gehrig's disease. With each visit, the window to Mitch's heart, which had closed gradually from years of cynicism and diminishing faith, was pried open through the wisdom and power of Morrie's indomitable spirit. Morrie taught Mitch to live every day is as if it was his last—that the only solution in life is love.

When I read this wonderful book, I was flooded with memories of a similar experience in my own life—regular weekly visits with a special mentor who transformed me as a coach and human being. These visits opened me to the possibility that there is something to value and admire in everyone, and that we may completely miss these qualities until we are truly present.

After I graduated from college, I spent the ensuing eight years completely immersed in my chosen career of coaching. I was so obsessed with building my swim team that I closed off nearly every other area of my life, withdrawing from friends and family as I relinquished any semblance of balance. There was only one small exception in my single-minded, all-consuming compulsion. Each Wednesday, as soon as I finished coaching morning practice, I headed east on the Ventura Freeway to the L.A. suburb of Encino to visit my mother's parents, Ruby and Ben.

The rewards that come from being fully present may not always be immediately apparent.

They were poor, living in a run-down apartment as they scraped by on the tiny stipend of their combined Social Security checks.

My grandfather, Ben Harrison Orkow, had been a writer his entire adult life. A big success in the twenties and thirties, he had been an acclaimed screenwriter and playwright living in Beverly Hills and rubbing shoulders with such stars of the day as Clark Gable and Cary Grant. But he had stubbornly refused to adapt his writing style and language to the changing world of the post-war years and lost every cent of his once sizable fortune.

My grandmother, Ruby, was a dazzling beauty of nineteen when she first met Ben, the sophisticated and brilliant writer. Having been raised in poverty, she was swept off her feet by his wealth, charm, and confidence. After a whirlwind courtship they were married, certain that a life of affluence, glamour, and success lay ahead. A year after they were married, they welcomed a beautiful little girl into the world and named her Miriam. They were elated about their baby, who grew up to be my mother.

But their carefree joy was short-lived. As my grandfather's fortune and reputation plummeted, Ruby was forced to take a job as a salesperson at a woman's clothing store. Ben steadfastly refused to pursue any other employment to help with their dwindling finances and continued to pour out manuscripts, plays, and screenplays that drew rejection after rejection.

There is something to value and admire in everyone.

Every day, Ruby worked at the clothing store, rushing about on her feet for eight to ten hours, only to return to a house that needed cleaning, a husband impatiently awaiting his dinner, and a daughter who needed the love and presence of a mother too exhausted to deliver. Gradually, Ruby developed more and more dependence on alcohol to escape her frustration and fatigue.

Over time the marriage diminished into empty coexistence. Ben had married Ruby for her beauty and charming innocence. He had envisioned her as the perfect hostess for celebrity dinner parties and as his companion for gala evenings in Hollywood and New York. But, as the strain mounted and Ruby's physical beauty faded beneath lines of worry and weariness, Ben never looked beyond her physical appearance nor opened his heart to feel her pain. With understanding and tenderness, he might have discovered her real beauty—her great wit and passion for life. But he never balanced romance with respect. They grew further and further apart as they lived separate lives held together only by the single focus and purpose they still shared—the love they felt for their daughter. But when Miriam left home at nineteen to marry and begin her own family, the walls between Ruby and Ben grew nearly impenetrable.

The gaping wound that was left when my mother moved away was partially healed when my sister and I were born. We became the new bright spots in my grandparents' otherwise lonely lives. To my grandfather, I was a shining star, and as I grew up, I looked up to him as a genius and my true idol. He had brilliant, creative ideas with an energy for learning that knew no bounds. A voracious reader and thinker, he rose every morning at four to devour every book he could put his hands on. When I was a boy, I was certain he was the smartest man who ever lived.

I viewed my grandmother quite differently. We had my grandparents over for dinner at least two or three times a month and for every holiday and birthday throughout the year. Ruby continued to be the breadwinner, working full time into her late sixties while my grandfather kept writing without results. Inevitably she would arrive at family dinner parties already tipsy from nipping at her bottle of vodka as soon as she returned from the store, and then would proceed to have another couple of cocktails before we sat down to dinner. I knew nothing about her alcohol addiction at that time, so I just assumed she was bizarre—gentle and affectionate—but scatter-brained and basically wacky. I built a superficial rapport with her, clowning and joking to make her laugh, but without really knowing her, loving her only out of duty.

Two things about Ruby puzzled me, though. They didn't seem to fit the loony-tune picture I had created of her. The first was her hands. Ruby had the gentlest, most expressive, and wisest hands I had ever known. When she spoke, her hands painted beautiful images in the air filled with emotion and delight. And when she touched me to rub my back or hold my hands, the effect was hypnotic. Love flowed through her fingers like the touch of an angel. The purity of heart that softly radiated from her hands brought me instantly to a place of peace that let me know there was somebody who loved me unconditionally.

The second anomaly came once each year on Christmas day. This was the one day I saw Ruby in the morning—the early morning. As a youngster, I was so excited about Christmas I pleaded with my grandparents to arrive at our house by 6 A.M. so we could begin to open packages. From the moment she walked in the door each Christmas dawn, it was as if a completely different person had stepped into Ruby's body. It was the one day her being seemed to perfectly match her hands. On Christmas, I loved my grandmother for who she was rather than out of a sense of familial obligation. She was like an angel each December 25: light, vibrant, and positively radiant. I felt a peacefulness and wisdom about her that day that blended perfectly with her warmth and affection. The effect was irresistible as she nurtured rather than smothered. Looking back now, this transformation in my grandmother each Christmas day meant more to me than any present or holiday treat. It remains my most precious Christmas memory.

When I went away to college, much to my surprise, it was Ruby's letters that I looked forward to more than any others. The packages she sent were filled with all sorts of delightful treasures. She had a knack for finding quotes, quips, or stories guaranteed to bring smiles. Her letters were filled with fun and energy. They almost seemed to glow when I pulled them out of my post office box.

Open your eyes to the beauty you can discover in the human soul when you learn to move beyond judgement.

After I graduated and settled into my new life as a coach, I decided that I would visit my grandparents every Wednesday morning. I would bring them their beloved delicatessen food, take them shopping, and make sure they had what they needed to get by until the next week. I'm not at all proud of the fact that I approached the visits as my duty as a "good grandson" and can see now I looked at them as a sort of noble sacrifice that would prove I was a truly giving person. Little did I know that I would receive far more from these visits than I could ever give. These Wednesdays with Ruby opened my eyes to the beauty we can discover in the human soul when we learn to move beyond judgment.

Week by week, I caught more glimpses of the pain and emptiness that had been my grandmother's reality for fifty years. It wasn't that she had been forced to work and carry the total financial responsibility for her family—in fact, she liked her work because it gave her contact with people and the opportunity to serve. Instead, her pain was the result of the daily tragedy of a relationship in which she was neither appreciated nor respected. Her husband saw her as a kind of flippety fool, incapable of meaningful conversation and substantive opinions. She lived without the most basic right of simple human dignity.

Through it all, my grandmother somehow continued to see joy where others saw routine, to find delight in simple, everyday things that others passed without the slightest notice. By taking the time to be present with her each week, gradually I began to appreciate her rare and special wisdom. And more and more, I found delight in her laughter. Ruby could let go and really laugh. How many of us have forgotten how to truly enjoy the gift of un-restrained laughter?

No matter the circumstances of our lives, we have the constant opportunity to choose joy.

One Wednesday about two years into my regimen, I sat down with Ruby after a short shopping trip, and we began to talk. As the conversation flowed, she bared her soul to me. That morning, my respect for my grandmother grew enormously. For the first time I finally began to see and appreciate her true spirit.

Early in her marriage, as Ben's career began to flounder, she'd tried to delicately make suggestions to him about finding a collaborator to help translate his ideas into language that resonated with the readers of the new day. Her attempts at encouragement had been cut off curtly, cast aside as the ignorant railings of a numskull. He'd made it painfully clear that her ideas and opinions meant nothing to him because he'd wanted her to understand her "place." So she'd learned to keep her thoughts sealed tightly inside.

We talked about many people in her life, and I was inspired by her positive attitude about others despite her own troubles. She didn't compare herself to others—she simply loved them. Ruby was almost egoless. When she talked about raising my mother, tears welled up in her eyes as she described how difficult it had been for her to be the disciplinarian in the family. It was not a role that came naturally to her, but she'd known that if she did not accept that responsibility, any semblance of discipline would have evaporated. My grandfather loved the image and ideal of parenthood, but Ruby was the one who rolled up her sleeves and dealt with the reality of keeping it all together. As she spoke, I marveled at her ability to communicate when someone actually took a moment to listen to what she had to say.

Whenever we are fully present for others we sing out to them that they are important.

Something else remarkable occurred to me that breakthrough Wednesday morning, because I realized that Ruby had stopped drinking. By simply having someone consistently there for her, she was being fed with love, and alcohol lost its luster.

The greatest human need is to be truly heard—to feel another's full loving presence—for it leads to genuine connection. Whenever we are fully present for others we sing out to them with unmistakable clarity that they are important! For the first time in ages, Ruby knew she was respected and genuinely special to someone. And for the first time, I realized how important Ruby was *to me*. I fell in love with my grandmother that morning, not out of duty, but for who she was.

Later, as I drove back to work I could not stop the tears. I cried because I had finally awakened to the intense pain my grandmother had endured—the ultimate pain of never being appreciated, admired, nor heard. I cried because I saw what a blind fool I had been throughout my life, looking only at her frailties and superficialities, never even suspecting there was a spirit of great beauty inside waiting to be invited out to dance. Most of all, I cried tears of gratitude, because I had discovered the truth about Ruby before it was too late. Over the next several years, my grandmother became one of the most important and influential coaches in my life, and my treasured friend. How fitting that her name was Ruby; she remains a shining example of the gem we can discover within everyone if we only take the time to be present and look deeper.

You cannot hope to bring out the best in others until you are fully present for them.

The visits with my grandparents lasted for eight years. Even after she died, Ruby continued to influence me, helping me learn lessons I have used often as a coach, parent, and teambuilder. One of the most important of these lessons was about *celebration*.

Ruby celebrated every delicious morsel of life— from bagels covered with cream cheese and strawberry jam to postcards from old friends and supermarket coupons she could use to buy products she enjoyed. She helped me recognize the immeasurable passion we bring to our lives through the power of celebration. And it was so much fun celebrating with her! From my visits with Ruby, I began to understand that one of the most powerful ways to build teams is to create moments of celebration.

But it wasn't until she passed away that the importance of celebration hit me full force. Until then, I had always avoided funerals, thinking of them as unnecessary events of sadness and pain. When Ruby passed away, my parents chose to hold no services of any kind for her because they shared that same view of funerals. But the more I thought about Ruby and the way she relished every precious moment, I began to see that we could choose to make the occasion of her passing a celebration of her life rather than a mourning of her death. In this new light, the idea of a funeral took on an entirely different meaning to me.

One of the most powerful ways to build teams is to create moments of celebration.

The night after Ruby passed away, I sat down with my wife and daughter Kelsey in front of our fireplace. I placed one of my most prized treasures above us on the mantle, a photo of Ruby as a nineteen-year old beauty. Around us I gathered the letters she had sent me in my Stanford days. They were so special to me I had saved every one. As we warmed ourselves by the fire we read them together and laughed—letting go of the sadness of her passing and instead celebrating the gift of her life. I shared many special memories from my Wednesdays with Ruby that night with my family. When we finished reading and talking, we looked up at Ruby's lovely face in the photograph.

Suddenly we sensed her presence and felt her gentle touch softly letting us know she would never leave us.

Whenever I have the opportunity to serve others as a coach, dad, husband, friend, or leader, I remember the lessons Ruby taught me. She, as much as anyone in my life, taught me to look for the possibility in others rather than the limits. She helped me understand that no matter the circumstances of our lives, we have the constant opportunity to choose joy. Her example made me aware of the power of celebration to bring people together. And, most of all, she showed me that you cannot hope to bring out the best in others until you are fully present for them. That simple truth is the cornerstone of coaching excellence.

Look for the possibility in others rather than the limits.

Ruby celebrated every delicious morsel of life.

Enjoy quiet moments of full presence with yourself.

chapter twelve

Yes, There's Even Time for You!

As vital as being fully present with others is to developing wonderful relationships and having positive impact on those around you, **being fully present with *yourself* is just as crucial to finding the ongoing peace of mind and spiritual energy required to coach effectively.** A simple analogy I discovered as a swim coach helps us understand the gifts we receive from quiet moments of full presence with *ourselves.* The analogy reveals a principle essential to balance and excellence called *recovery.*

To be a champion freestyle swimmer, you must develop optimum mechanics in the underwater portion of the armstroke, which is known as the "resistance" phase. Under water, you use a sculling motion to accelerate the maximum amount of water pressure you pull through. The resistance phase begins when your hand enters the water with the catch in front, and ends with a pushing release of water behind you, below your hip. This action is what propels you through the water and is the focal point for coaches and swimmers as they seek to improve performance. Most stroke technique suggestions from coaches aim at increasing efficiency in the resistance phase and pulling more water.

The resistance phase is like the "doing" parts of our lives—the initiative, personal power, and action we take to power through each day. However, there is a more subtle yet equally important phase in every complete armstroke. This is the portion of each stroke that occurs *above* the surface, just after you release the water behind you, and it's called the "recovery phase."

By developing our recovery phase, we find a reserve of strength that empowers our spirit.

During this portion of the armstroke, you lift your elbow behind you then reach out in front to catch the water for the next armpull. It is in the recovery phase that swimmers must relax, refuel, and replenish.

No matter how powerful we are during the resistance phase, without an efficient recovery on each stroke, we will rapidly wear down. We will weaken, and eventually our performance will diminish. But with an effortless recovery we more than endure; we flourish.

The recovery is the "being" part of our lives—the perfect metaphor for quiet moments of peace when we give ourselves the opportunity to replenish. At first, recovery may not seem as spicy and flavorful as resistance, but in the long run it is more nourishing. By developing our recovery phase, we find a reserve of strength that empowers our spirit and manifests emotionally as confidence and spiritually as faith.

The next time you watch a great athlete or performer, tune in to the recoveries. I always marveled at how

Michael Jordan used his "off switch" just as smoothly and efficiently as he used his "on." He wasted no energy when he had the opportunity to rest and recover. He never worked against himself. It was one of the secrets of his exceptional durability. With his finely tuned recovery skill he was always ready to explode to the basket or make the big defensive play when he was most needed.

You can develop the same skill so you are ready to give your best when you are most needed. Begin today! Take the time to replenish. Don't wait. Make it a daily habit as automatic and important as eating. Go for a walk in the woods, sit in the sunshine, or let the rain fall gently on your face. Take ten slow, deep breaths and truly relax. Spend time each day in prayer, visualization, or meditation. Get quiet. Write in your journal. As you develop the habit of giving yourself quiet recovery time each day, you will discover that in the moments we are fully present with ourselves, we allow ourselves to be in the loving presence of the ultimate coach who guides us all, God. In these moments you will feed your soul.

Take the time to replenish. Don't wait. Make it a daily habit as automatic and important as eating.

"I vowed to see the beauty in life, and appreciate every second that's mine."
-*Cheryl L. Costello-Forshey*

chapter thirteen

Taste Life's Dessert: Become Alert! (Heaven Can't Wait.)

One evening as we dined in a cafe in the Bitterroot Valley of Montana, my youngest daughter, Jenna, opened my eyes to a secret of extraordinary coaching and leadership I had nearly forgotten. The cafe was located on the second floor of a old main street building and had huge windows that captured the stunning panorama of the Bitterroot and Sapphire Mountain ranges enclosing the valley. Everyone in the cafe was eating or chatting quietly when something caught Jenna's attention and she walked over to the window. As she stood gazing out at the mountains, suddenly her eyes brightened and a look of pure wonder came over her. Then, with great excitement and considerable volume she announced for all to hear as she pointed out the window, "Look, Mommy and Daddy. We're in *heaven!*"

Everyone in the restaurant lit up at her revelation. The more I thought about it, the more I realized Jenna was right. She had seen and felt the beauty that is always around us, but that most of us pass without the slightest notice. We can miss the "heaven" that is right before our eyes. Yet opportunities abound in our lives when we remember to look for them.

Great leaders and coaches are extraordinarily alert because they recognize that sometimes the smallest insight can make the biggest difference. Each Monday during the last thirty-five years of his remarkable life, Mahatma Gandhi did not speak. He made this choice for religious reasons, but found it had an amazing and unexpected effect. These silent Mondays helped Gandhi to heighten his powers of observation, to let go of defensiveness and the need to be right. Most important, never once on these days of silence did he find himself thinking about his response when another was speaking. Instead, he was truly listening. Gandhi's choice created the opportunity for him to develop keen alertness and sensitivity. You can build this same skill by quietly disciplining yourself to use your own senses to take in information more fully.

Gandhi's silent Mondays created the opportunity for him to develop keen alertness and sensitivity.

In college I enrolled in a class called "Observation of Children." It was held once a week at a preschool located on the Stanford University campus. Each of us selected a child to be our subject for the eleven-week quarter. Our task was simple: We were to observe everything we possibly could about our chosen child during our three-hour session each week. At the end of the quarter, we were to write a paper detailing our observations and thoughts from the experience. While observing we were not to speak to our subjects, and we were instructed to remain as inconspicuous as possible. The children were accustomed to having college students milling around, so the challenge of becoming invisible was not as difficult as one would think.

To be honest, I had enrolled in the class only to complete the developmental psychology units I needed for my major. I thought it would be a simple course, a break from the rigorous schedule I was facing that quarter. Little did I know that it would become one of the most stimulating educational experiences of my entire college career, and its impact would last me a lifetime.

Within minutes of observing the girl I had selected, I was completely enthralled. I watched her with total concentration. It soon became obvious to me that I had never really observed another human being with such sustained focus in my entire life. The three hours flew by so quickly they seemed like minutes.

How quickly most of us make judgements about one another and then hold onto our initial impressions.

The more I observed, the more I connected with this girl's spirit. I understood her perhaps as well as anyone I had ever known, though I never uttered a word to her. I watched her grow and develop over those eleven weeks in her language skills, physical dexterity, courage, and interpersonal relationships. It was like watching a flower blossom under time-lapse photography. I realized how quickly most of us make judgments about one another and then hold onto our initial impressions without gaining the greater insight available to us through expanded observation. If her teachers could have stepped into my shoes, they would have discovered so much more about what inspired her, built her confidence, and sparked her curiosity. I became acutely aware of how much I miss in most conversations with others because I am so occupied with my own thoughts about what I will say next.

When we use our senses more acutely and sharpen our alertness, we discover opportunities to affect and inspire others as never before. It is a surefire strategy to become a dedicated lifelong learner— an absolute requirement for coaching excellence.

Today, I carry a beautiful poem in my wallet to remind me of the impact we create when we use our awareness and our senses with our full potential:

The Most Beautiful Flower
by Cheryl L. Costello-Forshey

The park bench was deserted as I sat down to read
Beneath the long, straggly branches of an old
       willow tree.
Disillusioned by life with good reason to frown,
For the world was intent on dragging me down.

And if that weren't enough to ruin my day,
A young boy out of breath approached me, all tired
       from play.
He stood right before me with his head tilted down
And said with great excitement, "Look what I found!"

In his hand was a flower, and what a pitiful sight,
With its petals all worn—not enough rain, or too
    little light.
Wanting him to take his dead flower and go off to play,
I faked a small smile and then shifted away.

But instead of retreating he sat next to my side
And placed the flower to his nose and declared with
    overacted surprise,
"It sure smells pretty and it's beautiful, too.
That's why I picked it; here it's for you."

The weed before me was dying or dead.
Not vibrant of colors, orange, yellow, or red.
But I knew I must take it, or he might never leave.
So I reached for the flower, and replied, "Just what
    I need."

But instead of him placing the flower in my hand,
He held it mid-air without reason or plan.
It was then that I noticed for the very first time
That weed-toting boy could not see; he was blind.

I heard my voice quiver, tears shone like the sun
As I thanked him for picking the very best one.
"You're welcome," he smiled, and then ran off to play,
Unaware of the impact he'd had on my day.

I sat there and wondered how he managed to see
A self-pitying woman beneath an old willow tree.
How did he know of my self-indulged plight?
Perhaps from his heart, he'd been blessed with
        true sight.

Through the eyes of a blind child, at last I could see
The problem was not with the world; the problem
        was me.
And for all of those times I myself had been blind,
I vowed to see the beauty in life, and appreciate every
        second that's mine.

And then I held that wilted flower up to my nose
And breathed in the fragrance of a beautiful rose
And smiled as I watched that young boy, another
        weed in his hand
About to change the life of an unsuspecting old man.

In this moment of authentic, grateful receiving everyone could feel the connection to "giving and receiving" as one.

chapter fourteen

Want to be a True Giver?
Learn to Receive and Open Yourself
to Abundance!

Have you ever noticed how much easier it can be to give compliments than to receive them? It feels so natural and comfortable to tell others how terrific they look or how much you enjoy and appreciate them—but when kind thoughts are returned, you begin to wriggle and squirm like a fish out of water. Why have we become so uncomfortable about receiving?

The simple truth is that many of us have undergone some effective negative conditioning when it comes to receiving. From the time we were small, we were warned about such evils as getting a swelled head, becoming cocky or conceited, or thinking too much of ourselves. Often comparison was used as a powerful control mechanism to keep us in check. We heard such debilitating statements as, "Why don't you act more like your sister?" We were instantly reminded of our limits and our faults—that we would never fully measure up. For many, the end result of this conditioning is doubt about our worthiness that causes us to deflect compliments and gifts of spirit.

Yet when you break free from this conditioning and

dig deeper by asking a question, "What is receiving?" an entirely new awareness emerges. To really understand receiving, you must first acknowledge how it feels to give. Whenever I ask participants in my seminars, "How many of you *love* to give?" the response is unanimous. The feelings of love and connection that accompany acts of giving are among the most treasured in all of human experience. It feels so good to give.

To really understand receiving, you must first acknowledge how it feels to give.

With this fresh awareness about giving, let's return to the original question, "What is receiving?" Suddenly the truth is unmistakable—receiving *is* giving in one of its most important and empowering forms. **Receiving allows others to experience the joy of giving.** When we receive happily and gratefully, we enable others to enjoy the same loving emotions we relish when we give. We accept rather than reject; connect instead of separate. But if we turn away from others when they seek to give to us, if we "keep score" or refuse to receive unless we record an IOU that must be repaid, or fidget in discomfort and deny the sincerity of the giver's sentiment, we take away their joy. Moreover, we deny ourselves the gift of true abundance. **We will never feel abundant until we learn to receive.** Indeed, until we receive with openness and gratitude, we will find ways to miss out on some of life's greatest moments. But when we learn to receive easily and happily, we actually let go of ego and become shining examples of "we go!" It is one of the most easily forgotten secrets of outstanding coaching.

When Cuba Gooding, Jr. won the Oscar for best

supporting actor at the 1997 Academy Awards, he created an unforgettable moment for millions watching on television. It was his joy in receiving: Just as the football player he'd played in *Jerry Maguire* celebrated his moment of triumph, Gooding opened his arms wide to the world and exclaimed, "Yes! Thank you! Life is *good!*" In his moment of authentic, joyful receiving he gave everyone a huge lift and helped us understand that giving and receiving are one.

For most of my life, I had a terrible time with receiving. Though I desperately wanted to be loved and appreciated, I was mortified at the thought of appearing conceited and overly taken with myself. With these conflicting emotions, behind my generosity was always the secret motive of using it as leverage to receive adoration, but then I would push away the very admiration and acknowledgment I'd craved when it came my way, all so I could maintain my facade of humility. Crazy and convoluted, don't you think? I had squeezed myself between a rock and a hard place trying to appear the essence of unselfishness, while deep down inside I felt starved for attention.

It wasn't until my graduate school years that I began to accept the person I had become rather than constantly trying to prove myself. With this simple acceptance, I found it refreshingly easy to admire my classmates for their talents rather than continually comparing myself to them. I became involved in the school and student government with the most genuine and unselfish motives I had ever felt. I was alive, energized, and truly excited

When we receive happily and gratefully, we enable others to enjoy the same loving emotions we relish when we give.

about serving without any attachment to what I received in return.

As the president of the UCLA Graduate School of Management Student Association, I was responsible for organizing events and programs that created a sense of community in our hard-driving academic world. The student association was the vehicle for students to become involved in their areas of special interest through clubs and activities that helped them expand beyond the classroom. It was also a key mechanism for injecting some fun into a pressurized environment heavily focused on future professional pursuits. For me, the association provided the opportunity to build a genuine team among students with widely diverse backgrounds and areas of interest. I jumped in with both feet, encouraging and supporting my teammates with robust enthusiasm. We had a terrific year, created many outstanding events, and solidified the financial strength of the student association for future classes. These results were quite satisfying, but the real enjoyment came from working together to achieve goals in which we believed.

Real enjoyment comes from working together to achieve goals in which you believe.

One of my last duties as president was to participate in the committee that would nominate deserving students for the highest student award for leadership and service at the graduate school—the Dean's Award for Outstanding Service. Officers of the Student Association were not eligible for the award as we had already received considerable recognition for our roles in student government, ensuring that the award would go to an individual who served not for personal reward or position, but with a spirit of genuine volunteerism and desire to make a difference. I was excited about helping select the award winner and nominated five or six classmates I felt deserving of the honor. Once the final list of nominees was chosen, a team of students, professors, and administrators would decide upon the winner, who would receive the award during commencement ceremonies.

On graduation day I was seated on stage at UCLA's venerable Royce Hall because I was to present the Outstanding Faculty Award to a professor selected by vote of the students. As I sat gazing out at the sea of graduates, friends, and family joined together for this day of celebration, I felt a sense of accomplishment and completion. And when I spotted my beautiful fiancee directly across the auditorium from me in the balcony, I burst into a smile that would not go away.

Until we receive with openness and gratitude, we will find ways to miss out on some of life's greatest moments.

As the ceremonies drew toward the close, the dean rose and strode to the podium carrying a four-page speech he had prepared to award the highest student honor, the Dean's Award for Outstanding Service. When the dean was about a fourth of the way into his presentation, I nearly fell off the stage in shock—he was talking about me! I looked across the hall at my fiancee who was gleaming with excitement. The dean explained to everyone that the committee had decided they could not abide by the long-standing rule that made officers ineligible for the award, because they had never known of an individual who had given more service, more unconditional support for classmates, and more inspiration to the Graduate Student Association. They had unanimously voted to toss out the rule and give the Dean's Award for Outstanding Service to me.

I was beaming! For perhaps the first time in my life I allowed myself to receive fully. I felt an amazing combination of appreciation, love, humility, and peace because this award was so unexpected, so unsolicited, and yet so authentic because deep down inside I knew I truly *was* deserving. Joyful, I had given the award away and it had come back to me with even more joy. In that moment I caught a glimpse of a universal law: The true path to receiving is to give away the exact thing you want, without any attachment to the result of your giving.

The true path to receiving is to give away the exact thing you want, without any attachment to the result of your giving.

Years later, my children drove this principle home in a way I will never forget.

A few days before Christmas when Jenna and Kelsey were five and eleven years old respectively, they each received brand-new, crisp fifty-dollar bills from their godparents. Neither girl had ever even held such a large bill in her hands before, much less owned one, so when they opened their cards and found the treasure, they almost fainted. With eyes as big as saucers, they stared at those fifties as if they were a million dollars.

The next morning, Jenna came downstairs still holding her fifty-dollar bill and peeking at it every so often as if to make sure it truly was real. We had told her we were going to the mall that day to finish our Christmas shopping and she could buy anything she wanted with the money. As she walked toward me still intent upon her treasure, I smiled, thinking of the toys and dolls she must surely have been conjuring in her mind. That Christmas, Jenna was absolutely enthralled with the animated movie character, Anastasia, so I was certain she was going to tell me all the wonderful Anastasia goodies she could buy with her fortune. I just knew she was envisioning a fifty-foot-tall Anastasia doll! It was a treat for me to see her so happy.

But then my five-year-old daughter brought me to my knees. She said, "Daddy, I was thinking about the fifty dollars. I already have so many presents under the Christmas tree; I don't need another one. Maybe there are some children who aren't even going to get one single present and this money could make their Christmas special, too. Maybe there's someone who won't have any-thing to eat unless we help them. Daddy, can I give my fifty dollars to someone who won't have a Christmas unless we help?"

I knelt down beside my little girl who had grown such a big heart and hugged her as my eyes welled up with tears of love and pride.

Just then I noticed Jenna's big sister, Kelsey, standing a few feet away. And she wasn't saying anything! She had watched and listened to all of this quietly, and she was really proud of her younger sister, but to an eleven year old, fifty dollars has far more real meaning than to a five year old. It's tough to be noble when you know what you're giving up! To Kelsey that fifty dollars represented

The feelings of love and connection that accompany acts of giving are among the most treasured in all of human experience.

several months of allowance, and she had been dreaming of some big ticket items that were suddenly within reach.

As touched as we felt about Jenna's generosity, we didn't want to put any pressure on Kelsey to give away her money, too. The money was a gift for her to use any way she chose. She's a terrific person, and she deserved to pamper herself.

She gave the matter considerable thought as we shopped that day. When we reached the food bank in the center of the mall, Jenna skipped over to the attendant and, grinning from ear-to-ear, handed her the $50 bill. At that moment, Carole and I each felt a tap on our shoulder. Kelsey looked up to us and said, "There are a lot of things I'd like to buy with this fifty dollars, but none of them would make me as happy as Jenna looks right now. May I give my fifty dollars away, too?" The shocked expression on stunned volunteers' faces now holding one hundred dollars from two children was priceless. I know Carole and I have never had a better Christmas present.

If you want financial abundance, give generously without concern for what you receive back.

When we went home later that same afternoon, among the many Christmas cards we received was one from my Great Aunt Ruth and Uncle Joe. I smiled when I saw Ruth's distinctive handwriting, for I knew what was inside. Every Christmas Aunt Ruth and Uncle Joe sent a wonderful card to "Brian Biro and family" with a twenty-dollar bill inside. As I looked closer at the envelope that afternoon, however, I was surprised to see that it was addressed to Kelsey Biro. This sparked my curiosity and, shuffling through more of the cards, sure enough I found a second one from Ruth and Joe addressed to Jenna Biro. I called the girls over and they eagerly opened their cards. When they looked inside, they couldn't believe their eyes. There within each card was a brand new, perfectly crisp fifty-dollar bill! Giving and receiving had come full circle.

If you want love, give it away freely and without expectation of return. If you want financial abundance, give generously without concern for what you receive back. If you want forgiveness, learn to forgive. When these gifts come back to you, enjoy them fully. Service is love in action. Understanding this law strengthens your ability to be a coach who inspires confidence, loyalty, and unselfishness by being an example of unshakable faith.

If you want love, give it away freely and without expectation of return.

New choices will ignite new joy.

chapter fifteen

You Can Change Your Life!

One fine day, my friend Tom was relaxing on his patio thinking about his life after a long but satisfying day's work. *Wow!* he thought. *I am so lucky! I am living a great life!* He had a beautiful home overlooking the ocean in south Florida, a great job, and best of all, he was in love with a woman he intended to spend the rest of his life with.

At the time, his prime focus outside of work had been on his girlfriend's career. She was an up-and-coming singer, and Tom was her manager. For two years he'd sacrificed every spare moment with single-minded devotion to landing a recording contract for her. Earlier that afternoon he'd received the call they'd been dreaming of day and night. A top record company offered her a lucrative deal. They would sign within a week! As he sat there on the patio sipping an ice-cold beer, he thought things just couldn't get any better than this.

A couple of days later he was dealt a blow he never saw coming. The woman he loved had found someone else. She wanted Tom out of her life. Just like that it was over.

Her words hit him like a freight train.

A year later on New Year's Eve he was living in a one-room apartment with only his clothes, a futon mattress, and a television. The breakup had hit him so hard that he just limped away, leaving her the house and virtually all their other possessions. His life had deteriorated rapidly into emptiness. Listlessly he struggled to work each day only to return to the tiny apartment and the silence that had become his only companion. Refusing to see friends or family, he had become a social hermit.

It becomes easy to blame others and make excuses for their emptiness and misfortune.

That New Year's Eve as he sat alone in the darkness, he hit rock bottom. He could no longer live this way. Either he was going to end it all, or he would take back control of his life. As he teetered on the brink of suicide, a thought swept over him that would turn his life around. He decided then and there that he was going to make the next 365 days "The Year of the Tom"!

He made a pledge to himself that every single day he would take at least one action that would enhance his life in some way, like reading a book or listening to a tape that would help him in his career, spending quality time with a good friend, exercising, or attending a seminar or lecture on a subject in which he had interest.

He told his friends about The Year of the Tom and asked for their help. They had been so worried about Tom they were thrilled about his new spark. Several of them got together and brainstormed ways to help Tom. They came up with the inspired idea of forming the "Intergalactic Annum Society"— the official sponsors of

The Year of the Tom. The society's charter was to "oversee the distribution of annual control" by keeping in constant touch with Tom. They even hosted a black-tie party where they awarded him a special certificate for bringing fresh meaning to his life through The Year of the Tom.

As the year progressed, Tom began to realize that many people go through life feeling helpless and without direction just as he had when his girlfriend left him. They resign themselves to just getting by, wishing that something better would come along. They hope for love, inspiration, and abundance instead of creating it. This helplessness paralyzes them into believing they have no control over their lives and their happiness. It becomes easy to blame others and make excuses for their emptiness and misfortune. By creating his year of action and celebration, Tom accepted full responsibility for the quality of his life, and empowered himself with the confidence to change it.

Accept full responsibility for the quality of your life, and empower yourself with the confidence to change it.

By the end of The Year of the Tom, he had transformed his life in countless ways. He was engaged to a beautiful, intelligent woman who loved him unconditionally. He had been promoted to a management position and loved the new challenge and responsibility. He found he had enormous passion for coaching and leading others. He had so much energy, he even started a side business in his spare time that generated substantial extra income and introduced him to many new friends. But the most dramatic change in his life was his newfound faith in possibility. He understood that not only do we have choices about what we *do* each day, we also have the ultimate choice about the meaning we give to life's happenings.

There are times when you must take care of yourself before you can muster the energy and spirit to truly serve others. Indeed, the decision to create special moments in your *own* life can shake you free from the depths of depression, re-ignite your purpose, and rebuild sagging confidence.

None of us can be loved until we let ourselves be seen. None of us can be seen until we learn to love ourselves. Our *faith, attitude,* and *actions* determine the quality of our lives. When we orchestrate moments in our own lives each day with the goal to grow, we take charge of these pillars of possibility and initiate rather than wait for fulfillment. We understand that we alone create our own example, a pivotal realization we must discover to see through the eyes of a coach.

Our faith, attitude, and actions determine the quality of our lives.

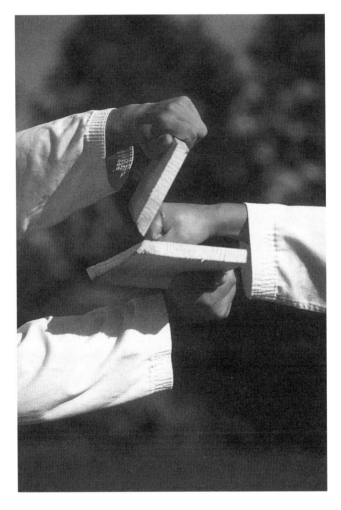

*All breakthroughs–physical, emotional, mental, and spiritual–
happen in a moment!*

chapter sixteen

Even if You're on the Right Track, You'll Get Run Over if You Just Sit There!

Some of the most unforgettable moments in my seminars on team building, possibility-thinking, and personal responsibility occur when participants break through a one-inch-thick wooden board karate-style. It's a personal metaphor for a breakthrough of real importance in their lives, so the energy and emotion that fills the room while it's going on is phenomenal. In our preparation for the breakthrough, we focus on several key beliefs that invoke new possibility. One of the most important beliefs is that *competency happens in a moment.* In board breaking, this means that even if you've tried to crack through the wood ten times without success, on the next attempt you have the potential to fly through the obstacle as if it were a piece of paper. The more you open to this belief, the more you access your true potential.

Just as in board breaking, the belief that competency happens in a moment gives us the confidence to persevere when faced with fears and obstacles, because we realize we alone control our own hope. A story about one of my closest friends demonstrates how perseverance is the primary quality we must instill in those we coach if we want to help them transform fear to freedom and failure to faith.

His nickname is "Hammer," and he stands about five feet and ten inches tall with arms the size of tree trunks— a friend you'd love to have beside you if you were in the tough part of town. No one would mess with you! But within that powerful frame beats a gentle heart. He sets the kind of example as a husband and father to which every man should aspire.

Competency happens in a moment; it gives us the confidence to persevere when faced with fears and obstacles.

I first met Hammer a few years ago when he phoned me and introduced himself because he wanted advice about becoming a professional speaker. We spoke at length, and when I hung up the phone I had an immediate intuition that this was a special person. I sent him my books and tapes with a note letting him know I'd be happy to help him pursue his dream in any way I could.

In the next several months I began to learn more about Hammer through several phone conversations. He was quite a story of perseverance and overcoming the odds. As a junior in high school, he'd weighed all of ninety-three pounds. (I saw a picture of him on the basketball team, and his tank top looked like an eight-person tent draped over his spindly body.) But his desire had been unflagging. Through pure effort and determination he had made his high school football and basketball teams. By the time he was a senior, he had worked himself up to almost 130 pounds and, thanks to a new coach who gave him his first real chance, Hammer not only became a starter, he became a star. He had improved so dramatically that he earned a football scholarship to a small college and eventually even tried out for the Dallas Cowboys.

Hammer took that same indomitable spirit that had served him so well in athletics and applied it in all areas of his life. He had never really focused diligently in school, but when he found and married his soulmate, Helen, he discovered a purpose that was bigger than himself. In their first seven years of marriage, he and Helen brought four beautiful children into the world. For the first time, he hit the books hard and earned his MBA while working full-time, determined to give his growing family financial prosperity. He put his perseverance to work by excelling in computer sales, rapidly climbing to the top at Toshiba and later at Texas Instruments. Though he was recognized as one of the elite salespeople in his field, and despite earning an outstanding income, his dream of speaking professionally and inspiring others continued to burn.

Hammer took that same indomitable spirit that had served him so well in athletics and applied it in all areas of his life.

Each time we spoke, I felt more compelled to do whatever it took to support him in realizing his vision. One day he called and asked if I would teach a one-day seminar for a company with which he had developed a close relationship. He was excited because he felt it would give him a great opportunity to study my program and style first-hand. When we met at the event we felt like old friends, though it was the first time we had actually seen each other face-to-face. The seminar was a great success, and seeing Hammer's special energy and talent that day, I became even more committed to helping him achieve his dream. Largely because of him, I decided to conduct my first "train-the-trainer" seminar.

Hammer was brilliant in the training, soaking in every idea, skill, and principle in this intensive five-day program. I've never seen a student pick up such an enormous amount of information so rapidly. By the time we completed the course, I knew he was a superstar in the making.

Several months passed before we had a chance to work together again. We were reunited when we were asked to come back to present two full-day events for the company that had originally hired us. As the events approached, I began to wonder if Hammer's enthusiasm for speaking had waned because of his skyrocketing success in computer sales. He had recently been recruited by one of the giants of the computer industry and given an outstanding compensation package. But any questions I had about his desire were answered in about thirty seconds when we saw one another. He was hungrier than ever to make the leap.

By the time we completed the course, I knew he was a superstar in the making.

By this time, my seminar business had grown through word of mouth to the point that I could no longer conduct all the events for which I was wanted. As we began a new year, I was able to line up two events for Hammer I could not fit into my schedule. It was the big break we had been waiting for.

About two weeks before the first of these events, Hammer flew out to Asheville, North Carolina (where I live) so I could work with him in an intensive day-and-a-half review session. When he arrived, we set right to work preparing for his program. What I didn't know at the time was that Hammer had been unable to study or review the material for months. His schedule with the new computer company had kept him working seventy-five- to ninety-hour weeks right up through the holidays, and he spent what little time he had left with his family. He was running on fumes when he arrived. Though excited, he was burned out from lack of sleep and worried because of his lack of preparation. He told me he was really pumped, but also pretty scared.

Despite these challenges, Hammer shined throughout the morning of the first day of the training. He has an amazing gift for humor and had me rolling on the ground laughing several times. I felt really confident about him as we planned his upcoming seminar. Things were going so well that we even added an inspirational story about his son, Cale, that was a perfect new addition to the program.

Perseverance transforms fear into freedom and failure into faith.

That afternoon I decided to raise the bar and told him he had about twenty minutes in which to prepare a one-hour seminar. At that point, I still didn't realize he had not had time to study the material. And Hammer has such a desire to please, he wasn't going to tell me. He didn't want to let me down. As I look back now, I should have been more perceptive and sensed the tension that swept over him when he received the assignment. Normally he would have been fired up about this kind of challenge. I should have seen that he was becoming more worried and uncertain by the minute. But my faith in Hammer was so strong I assumed he would pull this off without a hitch.

After twenty minutes of panicked preparation he

began his one-hour presentation with me as his audience. For about half-an-hour he flowed along nicely. But at that point he began to tighten up. As he tried to remember what to say, his self-doubt snowballed. The last half-hour was painful to watch as he struggled and faltered. When the time was finally up, he was so embarrassed and defeated in his own mind, he looked like a boxer who had just tried to take on Muhammad Ali in his prime. Frustrated and scared, Hammer found himself doubting if he would ever be able to live his dream. This was especially tough for him because as gentle, forgiving, and sensitive as he is to everyone around him, he is exactly the opposite with himself. Suddenly he found himself face to face with his greatest fear—humiliation—when he tried to picture himself as a speaker.

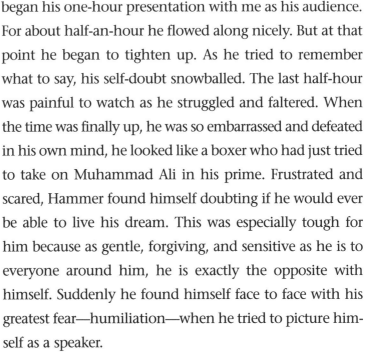

Champions have failed many more times than those who never approached their potential.

I did my best to console my nearly inconsolable friend, but made it clear that I believed in him every bit as much as ever. When you fall off a horse, you must get right back on if you want to be a great rider. Champions share a special secret about their success: They have failed many more times than those who never approached their potential. But they always see failure as temporary, their purpose and desired outcomes inevitable. As the great ice hockey player, Wayne Gretzky, said, "I've missed one hundred percent of the shots I never took." Champions keep on firing. I told Hammer he would have the rest of the evening and a couple of hours the next morning to prepare, but I wanted him to step up to the plate and give it another go.

As I left him that evening, I saw a man standing right

at the edge between fear and freedom, between failure and faith. If he retreated into the safety of his comfort zone he would still have a highly successful career in computer sales, a beautiful family, and much for which to be grateful. Yet, unless he jumped into the challenge zone, his dream would remain unfulfilled—and he would always know his fear had stopped him. Every fiber of my being told me Hammer had what it took to succeed, but as much as I wanted to give him that confidence, I knew the choice had to be his.

As much as I wanted to give him that confidence, I knew the choice had to be his.

That night when Hammer called Helen, his emotions spilled out. He told her how afraid he was, how much he doubted he could ever make it as a professional speaker. She gave him all the love and reassurance she possibly could, but hung up the phone deeply worried about her husband. She prayed intensely for him late into the night.

They did not know it, but they were together spiritually through that night, for Hammer, too, spent hours deep in prayer.

The next morning Hammer was up at 5 A.M. studying and practicing. He was scared to death and still battling his self-inflicted feelings of humiliation and embarrassment, but somewhere deep inside he had found the heart to rekindle his determination. At 8 A.M. he told me he was ready. I sat down to watch him, hoping the smile of confidence I attempted sufficiently masked the rumbling anxiety I felt in my gut.

One hour later I felt like the director, James Cameron,

on the night *Titanic* swept the Oscars at the Academy Awards. Hammer was phenomenal! He had me laughing, crying, and totally inspired every second of the presentation. It was a complete transformation. Though he knew he had improved dramatically, he had not yet learned to accept his own triumphs with the same enthusiasm he poured out to others. Yet, from the small smile he allowed himself, I could see he knew he was back on track.

When she'd heard it, she'd known the story was a gift from God just for Hammer.

On his way home at a connecting airport that afternoon, Hammer called Helen to let her know what had happened and that he was feeling better. She felt so relieved when she heard the spark back in his voice. She had been hoping and praying he would call, because she couldn't wait to tell him a story the minister had shared at church that morning. When she'd heard it, she'd known the story was a gift from God just for Hammer. It was a story of perseverance and the triumph that comes when you stay with your dreams.

When it comes to perseverance and overcoming the odds, Hammer's indomitable spirit keeps him in pursuit of his dreams.

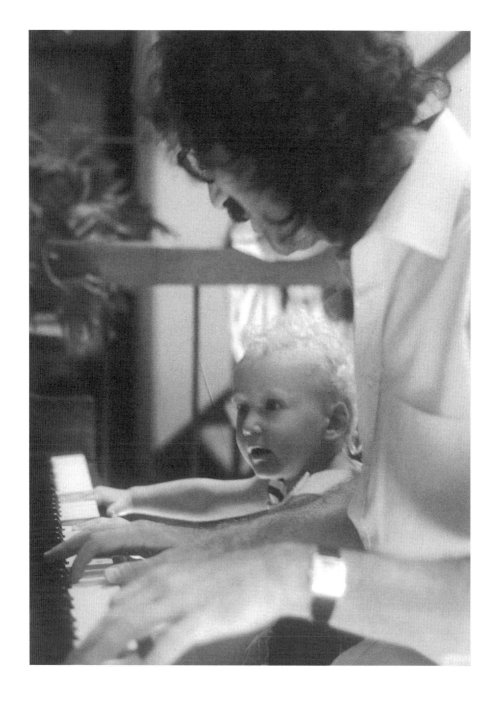

chapter seventeen

Don't Stop! Keep Right On Playing and Make Your Life a Masterpiece.

Helen's minister had told the congregation about a family, a mother and father who loved music and did all they could to encourage their four-year-old son to share their passion. They had started him with piano lessons when he was three years old, and he had already demonstrated some real potential. When they heard that a renowned pianist would be performing in their city, they decided to buy three tickets and to expose their son to the excitement of a live concert.

When they arrived at the auditorium, the air was charged in anticipation of the performance. Minutes before the performance was to begin, they bumped into some friends in the foyer and began chatting. The adults became so immersed in the discussion that they didn't notice that their son had wandered ahead into the concert hall.

Once inside, he spotted the beautiful ebony piano up on the stage. Guided by the innocent belief that pianos are for but one purpose—playing—he pranced up to the edge of the stage, found some stairs and proceeded straight over to the piano bench. Then, without a care in the world, he started playing "Chopsticks" just like he did for his mommy and daddy.

At first the audience who had settled into their seats was amused. But when the little boy kept playing and no one appeared to lead him away, a rumble of disapproval and irritation began to spread. "Where are his parents? How could they be so irresponsible? Someone get him off the stage!"

By this time the boy's parents had noticed that their son was gone and rushed into the auditorium in search of him. When they looked up on stage their panic evaporated, for there was their son, merrily playing his first major concert! It didn't take long for their relief to turn to embarrassment, however, as they sensed the audience's growing disapproval.

Just then, the master pianist walked quietly out and joined the boy at the piano. He, too, had heard the agitated crowd.

All the while, the boy had been so intent with his rendition of "Chopsticks" that he hadn't noticed the ruckus, so he was surprised when he felt the pianist's hand gently touch him on the shoulder. At first he was startled and wondered if he had done something wrong. But when the pianist smiled at him, leaned over, and whispered, "Don't stop. Keep right on playing," the child grinned and set to it again with renewed enthusiasm. Without another word, the pianist reached both arms around the boy and began to play right along with him. Suddenly, the familiar

But when the pianist smiled at him, leaned over, and whispered, "Don't stop. Keep right on playing," the child grinned and set to it again with renewed enthusiasm.

tune was transformed as the virtuoso joined the boy, adding harmonies and complementary melodies that filled the concert hall with magic. Every so often the pianist would lean close to the boy to say, "Keep right on playing! Don't stop!" The boy was having so much fun he was happy to oblige.

When they finished, the pianist gently took the boy's hand, and without a word, led him to the front of the stage. Smiling, hand in hand, they looked out at the packed house and bowed together, thoroughly enjoying the loud applause. The pianist dropped to one knee, hugged his young accompanist, then walked him to the stairs into the loving arms of his mother and father.

Sometimes your most treasured dreams are the most frightening.

When Helen had heard the story, she was sure it was a direct message from God telling Hammer to *keep on playing.* Before she'd gone to church that morning, she'd been terribly worried. In all the years she had known him, Helen had never heard Hammer as down as he had sounded that night on the phone. She had prayed all night long that he would not relinquish his dream and retreat to the safety of his comfort zone, a career in which he knew he could excel, but would never love. In her prayers she'd asked God for a way to help her husband, who was always so strong for others in times of need. Hearing the story had transformed Helen, and she'd known instantly that she had been given the perfect way to reach into Hammer's heart and rekindle his faith. She related the story with so much love and enthusiasm that he was moved to tears. As he listened, he realized that he alone controlled his own hope.

When he hung up the phone, the fatigue and pent-up emotion of the past twenty-four hours finally caught up with Hammer, and he started crying like a baby right there in the airport. Just then, an elderly woman happened by and saw him. Concerned, she offered him a tissue and asked if he was all right. Between sobs, Hammer managed to say thanks, took the tissue, and blurted out, "I love my wife so much!"

When we decide to persevere, we "keep on playing" the symphony we were born to perform.

The woman was so touched, her eyes filled with tears, too. Hammer reached out his powerful arms and gave her a huge hug. There they stood in a crowded airport, strangers only seconds before, but now connected as they shared a moment of simple human kindness.

As we coach and guide others, we must remember that sometimes their most treasured dreams are the most frightening. They mean so much that the thought of falling short, of not having what it takes, can be paralyzing. Doubt can sweep into their spirit and, if they allow it, can cause them to give up on themselves in the crucial moment when the fear reaches its pinnacle. But in that same moment, if we help them persevere, they hold the key to turning their dreams into reality. When we decide to persevere, to "keep on playing" the symphony we were born to perform, we hold the key to transform fear into freedom, failure into faith.

Through the eyes of a coach, you'll see others' greatness the instant you believe it.

chapter eighteen

When You See the Best, You'll Ignite It!

When we give unbridled passion, spirit, and effort to a worthwhile goal we step beyond the comfort zone into the challenge zone. It is in this uncharted territory that we open up the possibility to overcome a lifetime of fear and doubt. **In the challenge zone we position ourselves for truly extraordinary moments of inner triumph where real transformation can occur.** Coaching is all about facilitating this kind of transformation.

I had the unforgettable experience of working with an athlete who found the courage to move into the challenge zone. Our relationship taught me that only when you see the best in others do you have the chance to inspire it.

Throughout his swimming career, Ron was the kind of young man who caused coaches to shake their heads in disappointment and throw their hands up in frustration. Blessed with considerable natural ability, he skated by, never digging deep to bring out his true potential. His attendance record at practice was as unpredictable as the weather. Just when you'd begin to think he had turned the corner in his commitment, he would disappear for days at a time, negating any progress he'd made in conditioning and focus. He had enough talent to do pretty well even with his halfhearted effort, and he was friendly and easy going, never confrontational nor angry. He simply didn't seem to care that much.

Ron joined my team as he was about to enter his senior year in high school when he and the rest of his former club merged with ours to create a real United States Swimming powerhouse. I had seen him at meets over the years and knew of both his talent and his reputation for lackadaisical training habits. What I didn't know, when he walked onto the pool deck one September afternoon, was that buried beneath Ron's happy-go-lucky exterior beat the heart of a champion. There was a spirit of passion and energy within him just aching to come out. He was just frightened, like all of us when we hide from our possibilities. What if he gave his best, and it wasn't good enough? What if he committed himself and failed? It was so much easier to amble along on talent alone, protected by the invisible comfort zone called "unrealized potential."

Ron's past coaches had tried to needle him into caring, a strategy that clearly did not work over the long term. Occasionally, he would respond with an "I'll show you!" effort, but quickly he would slide back even further into his blasé attitude.

I have never believed in sarcasm as a motivator because the energy it evokes comes from embarrassment, fear, or revenge. These emotions can generate short-term results, but not long-term, thriving inspiration. From the

He was just frightened, like all of us when we hide from our possibilities.

moment Ron joined our team, I focused on his potential and praised him for every effort that moved him a little closer to it. When it comes to coaching, what you focus on is what you create. You must see what's possible in the people you coach, even when they don't see it themselves.

After his first week with the team, Ron came to me after practice and said, "Coach, I'm having fun here. You really believe in me, don't you?"

I responded, "Ron, you've been a joy to have here this week. You've got everything it takes to be the CIF champion if you decide it's something you truly want. You could have an amazing senior year. The greatest fun in life is to put your heart and soul on the line one hundred percent and to discover what's really inside of you. I *do* believe in you, and I'm really excited to be your coach."

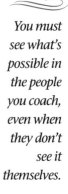

You must see what's possible in the people you coach, even when they don't see it themselves.

He smiled and turned just a tad red. But I could see the positive impact of the faith I had expressed in him far overpowered any embarrassment he felt receiving such big compliments.

After that talk, Ron became a dream for me to train. In all my years of coaching, never had I worked with an athlete who tried harder and had more fun doing it. Many of my athletes were incredibly hard-working, but so often these dedicated kids were extremely tough on themselves emotionally. They would hang onto one poor practice or performance, completely forgetting weeks of outstanding efforts. But when Ron made the decision to go for it, he placed his full faith in me *and* in himself. On the rare occasions when he didn't have his usual snap and power, he never let his positive spirit dissipate. As a result, he had few subpar days and bounced back from any disappointment almost immediately. More than any swimmer I'd ever had the pleasure to coach, Ron looked inside himself to determine his success rather than evaluating himself by what everyone else thought or what happened on the outside. Even on days when he didn't turn in his fastest practice times, he was able to feel good about his effort. With this fresh, unbridled spirit, Ron improved dramatically.

In simply making decisions and taking action you have already succeeded.

By the time the high school season began, Ron was performing workout sets and drills I had never seen accomplished before. And he loved every minute of it. He came to practice each day with a smile on his face and a twinkle in his eye that seemed to say, "Come on, Coach, let's see what we can do today!" Where years of cajoling and ridiculing him had left him uninspired and uncommitted, he responded to praise and positive energy with boundless enthusiasm.

His attitude and effort had quite an effect on the entire team. For the first time in his life, Ron knew what it felt like to be admired. He became our team leader because of his extraordinary example. His enthusiasm was infectious, and all of the kids seemed to have more bounce in their steps and worked harder while complaining less. Practices had never been so much fun.

It was hard to believe how swiftly the year had flown by when we arrived at East Los Angeles City College for the California Interscholastic Federation High School

Championship prelims. Ron was to swim three events, the two hundred–yard individual medley (fifty yards of each of the four competitive strokes), the one hundred–yard backstroke, and a leg on his school's medley relay. With all my heart, I wanted this transformed young man to experience a moment of great triumph at his high school championship. He deserved no less.

The prelims were the qualifiers for the finals that would occur three days later. Because of his fine performances during the dual meet season, Ron was seeded in the top three in both of his individual events, though there was no clear favorite. The top swimmers were closely bunched within a few tenths of a second of one another.

In the sport of swimming, top athletes train extremely hard. These determined kids rise each morning around 4:30 and hit the water by 5 A.M. for a two-hour workout before school. Then, after a full day in classes, they come back for an evening workout, another grueling two-hour test of stamina. On top of their endless hours in the pool, they lift weights four days a week. As a result, during the season, they are dead tired. The entire training strategy points at one shining light at the end of an exhausting tunnel—the taper and peak period. This is the three weeks or so before the big meet when they stop morning practices and gradually reduce the intensity of their afternoon workouts. With the added rest, their muscles and spirits begin to rejuvenate, and they prepare psychologically for their best performances. It is a very exciting time for a swimmer. With a couple of days to go before the target

When we give unbridled passion, spirit and effort to a worthwhile goal we step beyond the comfort zone into the challenge zone.

competition, the kids begin to feel so much energy they could pop! The last big step is to "shave down." The night before the big meet the kids shave the hair from their arms, legs, back, stomach—some even shave their heads, though most opt for a cap or a short haircut. When they hit the water after shaving they feel incredible—it's as if they are suddenly lighter than air. It's truly an amazing sensation and a huge boost mentally and emotionally.

For the preliminaries, Ron and I decided that he would not shave down. Though it was slightly risky, we felt confident he would easily qualify in the top eight anyway, and then would have an extra edge when he shaved for the finals.

The day of the prelims finally arrived and we were psyched! Ron's goal for the two hundred–yard individual medley was 1:57.9, and I secretly hoped that he might go as fast as 1:55.9 in the finals if everything went perfectly.

He had never broken 2:02 before, but we both were visualizing the best. In his preliminary heat he started off the race looking strong, but his timing seemed a bit off when he reached the breaststroke leg. The effort was there, but he

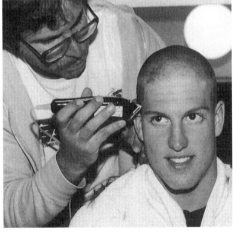

When they hit the water after shaving they feel incredible—it's as if they are suddenly lighter than air.

tired as the race progressed and really struggled the last twenty-five yards. His time was 1:59.9, and though it was a personal best, I could see his disappointment when he came over to me to talk about the race. Indeed, I was worried because he had really looked tired in the last half of the event, and the finals were only a few days away. He had worked so hard, and our hopes were so high, what if we had overestimated his ability? What if his goals were way out of reach? As he looked to me for answers, I could sense a tinge of doubt creeping into his mind.

I did my very best to instill more confidence in him than I actually felt at that moment. I smiled at him and said with great conviction, "You're still three days away. When the finals come on Thursday, you're going to be awesome!" Thank goodness he didn't know I was trying to solidify my own faith as much as his. True to the spirit he had shown all year long, he bounced right back as he listened to my brief pep talk, nodding at me with the twinkle back in those laughing eyes of his. He felt even better when we found out he had qualified first in the individual medley and second in the backstroke. But when we left the prelims that evening, I couldn't help but wonder if he was going to fall far short of his goals. He deserved his moment, and I prayed he would find something magical inside of him by Thursday.

That week at our short practices, Ron was right back to his cheerful, upbeat self. We both knew Thursday would be his one big shot at his dreams. If he approached the goals we had set for him he might even catch the eye

The rewards for living your word and holding tenaciously to hope and possibility cannot be denied.

of a college recruiter or two, with an outside chance of a scholarship. He would be a hero at his school—potentially a CIF champion—and single-handedly responsible for having his school earn an unprecedented top-five finish in overall team points.

Wednesday afternoon, after a very light practice with a few sprints tossed in to rev the kids' engines, I asked Ron to come into my office for a talk. He had been in my thoughts incessantly and I wanted him to know how honored I felt to be his coach. I wanted to thank him for the shining example he had set for our team. Even more, I wanted to thank him for all he had meant to me. Every day that season I looked forward to practice with extra enthusiasm knowing Ron was going to be there ready to meet every challenge with pure joy. I told him that no matter what he did the next day, he was already a champion in the truest sense.

Only when you see the best in others do you have the chance to inspire it.

"When you step up on those starting blocks tomorrow, remember how completely I believe in you. You deserve an amazing day and you are going to fly!" I gave him a big bear hug and joked with him about remembering to put a blade in the razor when he shaved down. The last thing I said to him was, "Sleep well tonight. You can rest easy knowing that you could not have prepared any better. You're ready!" As I watched Ron walk out to his car, I looked to God for help in making my "three days away" prediction after his prelim swims clairvoyant rather than unrealistically optimistic.

The energy was electric at the East L.A. City College

pool the next day. At that time southern California was the hotbed of swimming in the U.S., and the CIF Championships were the premier high school swimming event in the world. School spirit was running rampant as cheers erupted from every corner of the aquatic center. Only the fastest eight swimmers in each event had survived the preliminaries to make it to these finals, and each and every competitor was primed to put it all on the line.

Because I was Ron's United States Swimming coach and not his high school coach, I was not allowed on the pool deck for this championship meet. Knowing of this restriction, we had carefully gone over his warm-up plan in advance. I positioned myself at the most visible spot in the bleachers where Ron and all of my other swimmers could easily spot me. If it's possible to transmit energy and faith through space, from my perch up in the stands I sent my kids all I had as I watched them loosen up. I'd know quickly if it was to be a day of triumph or disappointment because Ron's first race, the two hundred–yard individual medley, would be one of the earliest events. I just hoped Ron wasn't as nervous as I was!

The instant you know you deserve the best, it is yours.

As he walked over to sit behind the starting blocks with the other seven competitors, Ron looked out at the end of the pool, deep in concentration. He was visualizing his race just as he'd done a hundred times. Each finalist stepped forward when introduced by the announcer and was greeted with a wild explosion of cheers. When Ron heard his name, he stepped up on the block and acknowledged the crowd with a wave, and then, spotting me, gave a quick nod as if to say, "I'm ready coach. I know I can do it!" I smiled back and gave him the thumbs up.

All cheering and last minute conversation came to an abrupt stop as the starter blew his whistle, the signal for total silence except for his instructions to the swimmers.

"Judges and timers ready—swimmers take your marks—"*Boom!* The gun went off, and eight peak-performance athletes exploded from the blocks, their legs driving like pistons as they stretched for the water. Ron had a terrific start, and within twenty-five yards he was already in the lead.

My heart nearly pounded out of my chest as I watched this tremendous young man find the brilliance that had always been hidden inside of him!

The first half of the race, consisting of the butterfly and backstroke legs, was his strongest, so I expected Ron to open up about a body-length lead. But when he hit the halfway mark I was stunned. He was flying! He was over two seconds ahead of the pace we had hoped for and had moved at least three full body lengths ahead of the second-place swimmer. I was excited, but could he keep it up?

I held my breath as he made the turn into the breaststroke leg. This was where he had faltered on Monday when his timing had fallen off and fatigue had crept into his arms and legs. But today, he looked fantastic! He was on top of the water, driving forward with terrific thrust from his whip kick. I had never seen him swim with such power in breaststroke before. My heart nearly pounded out of my chest as I watched this tremendous young man find the brilliance that had always been hidden inside of him! Fifty yards of freestyle left to go! I shouted in my mind, *Please let him finish strong!*

He turned for home, every muscle in his powerful body blasting toward the finish. With ten yards left, he put his head down and accelerated into the wall without breathing. His closest competitor was more than half a pool length behind him!

As soon as he hit the finish he whirled around to look up at the giant scoreboard clock that instantly flashed up his time: 1:53.86! He had shattered both the CIF record and exceeded our wildest dreams by more than two seconds. In the process, he had qualified for the most prestigious swimming meet in the United States, the Senior National Championships. We had never even considered that possibility!

As soon as he saw his time, he turned and looked for me in the stands. When our eyes connected he leaped out of the water to his waist and pumped his right arm toward the heavens in absolute joy and triumph. His huge smile was the greatest gift a coach could ever receive. The entire stadium was applauding wildly for him, and he flew out of the pool, forgetting all about my pre-race instructions to go straight into the warm down pool and loosen up for his backstroke event. Instead, he rushed up the stairs, pumping his fists and howling in utter delight until he reached me. He wrapped his arms around me and lifted me right off the ground in a giant hug of pure exultation. The next second, his parents joined our unrestrained celebration. Goosebumps, tears, and gratitude

When our eyes connected he leaped out of the water to his waist and pumped his right arm toward the heavens in absolute joy and triumph.

flowed nonstop. A phenomenal young man had transformed his life and received the moment he truly
deserved.

Ron went on to win the hundred-yard backstroke as
well, once again eclipsing the CIF record and demolishing
his personal best time by over two-and-a-half seconds. To
top it all off, he lifted his team on his powerful shoulders and
carried them to a third-place finish in the team standings, by
far the highest place they had ever achieved. Ron was
awarded the outstanding swimmer of the meet, and
received a full-scholarship offer from the University of Utah.

Your job as a coach is to fill those you serve—your business associates, students, children, and yourself— with this belief system centered on unconditional faith.

It's been said that God's delays are not God's denials.
Whenever we take actions in ways that positively and com-
passionately impact others; whenever we choose unselfishness over ego; whenever we give our most focused, dedicated, and determined efforts; our intent, energy, and
actions will lead irrepressibly to *deserved results* just as Ron
experienced. We may not find *instant* gratification, however.
Indeed, we may even begin to wonder, as time goes on, if a
lifetime of planting will ever result in a richly deserved
harvest. But when things seem the darkest, and your life's
circumstances the most unjust and unfulfilling, remember,
faith has no time limit. The rewards for living your word
and holding tenaciously to hope and possibility cannot be
denied. In simply making the decisions and taking action
you have already succeeded. The instant you know you
deserve the best, it is yours. You will experience joy that
cannot be taken away because, through your choices, you
will discover the healing, freeing peace of mind that is faith

in action. Your job as a coach is to fill those you serve—your business associates, students, children, and yourself—with this belief system centered on unconditional faith. Through the eyes of a coach, you'll see others' greatness the instant you believe it.

We have the capacity to lift those around us and transform even the most frustrating and stressful situations into opportunities for connection, new possibility and hope.

chapter nineteen

Communication When it Counts

It's been said that ninety-five percent of success is fail-ure. In my first book, *Beyond Success: The 15 Secrets of a Winning Life*, I suggested an empowering way to approach life's bumps and obstacles. Recalling a Thanksgiving church service I had attended in Anchorage, Alaska, I repeated the message the minister had delivered about dealing with stress and adversity. She'd said, "This Thanksgiving, I suddenly realized that perhaps we should give our greatest thanks for all the obstacles and setbacks we have faced along life's path, for it is from these that we have grown the most."

We and those we coach and love will meet with many challenges and disappointments. Our communication is never more important than during such times of turmoil and pressure. We have the capacity to lift those around us and transform even the most frustrating and stressful sit-uations into opportunities for connection, new possibility, and hope. The key is communication driven by an unshakable desire to serve.

The first and most often overlooked secret to effective

communication during times of stress is simply to do it! So often, when faced with the challenge of trying to say the "right" thing, we find it easier to say nothing at all. But effective communication is the steam valve that can ease the pressure from a boiling pot of emotion and stress. When we communicate from the heart, our genuine caring and positive spirit shine through. Communication driven by the desire to serve is our most powerful tool to demonstrate love, concern, and support.

When we communicate from the heart, our genuine caring and positive spirit shine through.

Years ago, at a time of deep sadness, I realized **that the love we fail to share is the only pain we live with.** Becoming a master of communication in times of stress enables you to take a huge leap toward living "pain free." So let's dive into several simple, actionable steps you can take to become an outstanding coach and communicator even during the most difficult of times.

Prepare those you coach for a future "aha!" by continuously planting seeds that will take root and sprout into conscious realization.

chapter twenty

View Your Communication as a Series to Make Your Ideas Stick!

Many of us think of communication as separate "bytes" of information, instruction, or motivation. But, to be a true master of communication, especially during times of stress, it is crucial to view your communication as ongoing. Each communication builds upon the previous ones and sets the stage for those to come.

This is particularly important to understand as a coach because of the way people make decisions. On average, a buyer of a product, service, idea, or opportunity will arrive at yes only after first rejecting your offer seven times. In other words, it takes seven noes to get to yes. The research goes on to point out one more startling truth. The average seller gives up after the third or fourth no. As a coach, you are selling ideas, strategies, and motivation. Often, your initial communication may serve primarily to plant a subconscious seed, preparing those you coach for a future "aha!" when that seed takes root and sprouts into a fresh, conscious realization. **When you view your communication as a series, you build a network of bridges connecting your key concepts and**

beliefs. You easily and purposefully restate your important messages in different ways because you know that people will grasp them at varying points along the connected communication pathway you have constructed.

Three tools are invaluable to support this series approach to communication. The first is *metaphor.* People love stories, even stories used to teach as they draw comparisons between something that is familiar and a new idea. More important, people open themselves to metaphors in the form of stories. The clergy use metaphorical stories to help us understand spiritual principles (for example, calling the body a temple to show how we must treat it), just as folk tales use metaphors to teach us about life. You can find metaphors almost everywhere you turn: in boardrooms, classrooms, and living rooms—wherever one human being wants to teach another.

Metaphors enable others to identify with your messages in their own personal ways.

When you use metaphors to express your important ideas and information, you delight and captivate rather than "data dump." You enable others to identify with your messages in their own personal ways. Metaphors are memorable and act like colorful threads weaving your communications together into rich tapestries. One of the great coaches in American history, Abraham Lincoln was a master of metaphor. Rarely did Abe give a direct order. Instead, he pulled from an almost endless bag of stories whenever he wanted to make an important point. The most striking effect of this approach was that not only did those listening to Lincoln *grasp* what he wished to convey, they took ownership of the ideas. Good stories have a way of settling into our subconscious and becoming *our* stories.

The second tool to employ in building your communication into an effective series is *summarization*. Though the information you seek to communicate may be crystal clear to you, it is probably new and unfamiliar for those you are trying to reach. When you summarize, you repeat your most important points simply and succinctly. The summary allows your messages to sink in at a deeper level and often brings fresh understanding to your original points. Your summary also becomes the perfect opening or "preframe" for your next communication.

Through enabling questions you move from talking to others to communicating with them.

The third and most important tool to connect your communications into an effective series is *enabling questions*. In chapter two, you learned that being a "master asker" is of huge importance in quality coaching. Enabling questions are those that assist others in becoming *fully associated* to experiences or feelings that have positive and constructive meaning for them. Through enabling questions you move from *talking to* others to *communicating with* them. You discover what they have gained and retained from

your previous communication and how they have used that information in their lives. By asking enabling questions of others and listening fully to their answers, you know where to begin your present communication. You step into their shoes and, as Stephen Covey expressed so beautifully, "seek to understand before you seek to be understood." When people feel listened to, they become far more ready to listen.

By asking enabling questions of others and listening fully to their answers, you know where to begin your present communication.

During times of stress and pressure, one of the most powerful coaching tools in your communication toolkit is a playful, surprising sense of humor.

chapter twenty one

Keeping Your Team Light With The Magic of Humor!

Once when Mahatma Gandhi traveled across India preaching peace and nonviolence, a band of crazed fanatics rushed at his train, brandishing spears and clubs, determined to stop the gentle giant by force. Despite the desperate pleas of his aides and supporters, the Mahatma peacefully stepped out onto the train platform and smiled kindly as he looked into the shocked faces of the wild horde. Then, quite calmly but with just a hint of playfulness in his voice, he said, "You have every right to disagree with me—but must you also break my head?" His humor in the face of intense danger was so unexpected, so unnerving to the attackers, the effect was like a needle puncturing a balloon inflated to the limit. The "hot air" flew out of them. They stopped in their tracks, lowered their weapons and quietly rode away.

During times of stress and pressure, one of the most powerful coaching tools in your communication toolkit is a playful, surprising sense of humor. Often the most important outcome you desire from your communication during times of stress is to turn the tide of negative emotion just as Gandhi deftly turned that frenzied mob. Fear, anger, and frustration are like those fanatics—they gather steam if unchecked by a voice that interrupts their surge. Humor is a magnificent show stopper. When you present an unexpected perspective with wit and humor, you immediately help others change their emotional state and access fresh resources.

Think back to the finest teachers or coaches you have ever known. I would wager that most of them recognized and used the extraordinary educational value of humor in their teaching. Great coaches know that the time to lighten up is when the team begins to tighten up. **One of the hidden secrets of using humor is its impact on attention.** Listeners maintain a higher level of focus and concentration when they suspect something unexpected and fun may pop up at any time. They tune in at a higher level trying to find out when! Education is most profound and effective when it includes a healthy portion of humor—especially when it is upbeat and without sarcasm. As a coach, you must remember that you *are* an educator, helping others discover new knowledge, often by breaking through old beliefs and biases that stand between them and fresh opportunity.

You don't have to be a stand-up comic to inject fun into your team. The secret is to surprise people by doing the unexpected.

You don't have to be a stand-up comic to inject fun into your team. The secret is to surprise people by doing the unexpected. When I was a swim coach and felt the team pressing too hard, I would occasionally stop practice, pick out one of the kids and say, "Repeat after me three times as loud and as fast as you can:

"One smart fellow, he felt smart.

"Two smart fellows, they felt smart.

"Three smart fellows, they all felt smart!"

(Try this yourself right now and you'll see what happens!) As soon as one would finish (undoubtedly having botched the attempt at the tongue-twister) I'd point to another and command, "Your turn! Go!" In rapid succession I'd choose another of the kids, and another, always exhorting them to speak louder and faster. The next thing we knew, everyone was laughing and having fun with each other. Fresh energy replaced the stagnation, frustration, or lack of focus that had infected us only moments before.

As a professional speaker I make a conscious effort to direct my humor good-naturedly at myself. I joke about my bungles and mistakes rather than teasing others about theirs. When my audience sees that I can laugh at my own humanness, it becomes easier for them to lighten up about themselves. With that lighter spirit they are much more inclined to open up and see themselves honestly so that they may make new and improved choices. In this way, a healthy dose of humor is the perfect tool to move from ego to "we go!"

When you present an unexpected perspective with wit and humor, you immediately help others change their emotional state and access fresh resources.

Four and five year olds at play often reveal one of the most underused, surprising and effective secrets of extraordinary coaching – the power of games!

c h a p t e r   t w e n t y   t w o

Get 'Em Off the Sidelines and Into the Game!

If you ever want to see creativity in action, there is one surefire spot you can count on observing almost unlimited innovative genius. It's better than most any art studio, movie set, or scientific laboratory. Have you guessed where this creative paradise is yet? Here's one major clue: The brilliant minds frequenting this think tank have generally not yet learned to read. You've got it now! Creativity central is none-other than your local preschool. To see no-holds-barred, sky's-the-limit creative thinking, spend one hour watching a group of four and five year olds at play.

These precocious Einsteins reveal one of the most underused, surprising, and effective secrets of extraordinary coaching—the power of games! Just like children, big kids (adults) love to play. And when we involve our teammates in play we can move them off the sidelines and into the game where they can discover opportunities, lessons, and breakthroughs that have eluded them in the all-too-serious "real" world.

Games are creativity creators. I have used them in

seminars to great effect for many years. Each game has specific insights that come out when we integrate what we've learned from the activities. **But just as important as the principles we derive from the games is the way they manage to move people from the sidelines into action.** Individuals who had been only semi-involved in the seminar immediately come to life when I introduce the first game. Their bodies, minds, and spirits become engaged rather than idle. That's the most fertile environment for real learning.

The fun and humor in games makes it easier for participants to laugh at themselves and to welcome fresh insights and ideas.

Games also serve to bring teams together in a unique way by creating a common direction and purpose. There are no individualized agendas during the games. Participants are focused on the supposedly simple objectives and try their best to work together to succeed. As they do, they learn to truly support each other, and spirit and appreciation begin to flourish. When the surprises and empowering principles are revealed at the end of the games, participants are open and upbeat rather than defensive. The fun and humor in the games makes it easier for them to laugh at themselves and to welcome fresh insights and ideas. This is exactly the same kind of energy you want to create in the realm of your business, family, or community.

In the bonus section at the end of this book, you will find detailed descriptions of two wonderful games you can use as a coach with your teams at work or at home. By investing a little time to facilitate these games, you will inject fresh vitality, inspire teamwork, and reap rich rewards for all involved as they put the important principles they've learned into action.

By giving my daughter the space to be herself, I began to enjoy her unique and sparkling spirit even more. Our love has grown from conditional and fragile to unconditional and unstoppable.

chapter twenty three

Give Space to Those Who Seem to Be Rejecting You and Energize Yourself!

Every day your patience and resolve as a coach will be tested, because coaching is the art of seeing the best in others when they do not see it in themselves. You will face no greater challenge as a coach, parent, and leader than rising above your need for approval. Sometimes the people you most wish to affect will seemingly reject you. Some will push back hard against your faith, your determination to hold them to higher standards, even your enthusiasm. Others will use every unconscious trick in the book to gain your attention. If you allow them to affect you, your energy will dissolve, and you may make decisions based not upon what is best for them and the team, but rather upon what you think will win them over to your side. The instant you find yourself motivated by the need for approval, you put yourself at the effect rather than the cause of your peace of mind as a coach. And, in many cases, the more you try to win approval, the less respect you will receive.

When I first began teaching seminars, I lived and died according to the evaluations I received from participants at the conclusion of the program. The second the last participant left at the end of the day, I would dive into the evaluations and devour every word. I wasn't looking for constructive suggestions for improvement, but rather for every superlative and statement of praise I could find. Because my events are vibrant, fun, and alive, the evaluations were almost unanimously positive. But every so often there would be one that said something along the lines of "pretty good," or "okay." If I received one of those blasé ratings, I was crushed. Why didn't they like me?

You will face no greater challenge as a coach, parent, and leader than rising above your need for approval.

At the same time, I began to notice that I seemed magnetically drawn to the one or two people in each audience whose body language said, "Skeptic here—keep away." It was as if my primary job was to win them over. Of course, the more I focused on these few, the less I gave to the many.

The most striking consequence of these two approval-driven actions was internal. When I finished teaching, I would find myself completely drained. I didn't want to see one more person. All I wanted to do was read the evaluations and crash.

One evening as I sat waiting to catch a plane after teaching an event in St. Louis, I finally realized that the real fun in teaching was disappearing for me because of my insatiable need for approval. I asked myself if I taught to receive adulation, or because I loved my work and felt that I was serving a higher purpose. From that day forward, I no longer asked for written evaluations. I rapidly found that if participants had suggestions they wished to share, they would come forward and offer the input without the formality of a written evaluation. If a participant or two appeared skeptical or uninterested during the event, I simply "gave them the space" to choose to accept or reject what I offered. With these new choices, I immediately felt an extraordinary increase in my own energy. When I finished teaching I would feel revitalized. For the first time, though I had taught for nine or ten hours, I loved connecting with the participants to sign books or to just be present with them. I also began to observe that the skeptics seemed to come around and to join in much more often. By letting them go, the push-back response was dissolved and they sensed that while I absolutely loved and believed in what I was teaching, they were free to accept or reject the principles as they saw fit. Given that free choice, most let their defenses down and became active, positive participants.

The instant the need for approval becomes our driving motivation, we become conditional coaches.

Later, the power of giving space in the face of possible rejection was put to an even tougher test for me as a father. In the first four years of my youngest daughter's life, she most definitely favored her mother. It's not unusual for infants to be especially drawn to their mother, but as Jenna began to walk and talk her disdain for me seemed to, if anything, increase. In fact, most every day, her rejection of me was so obvious it is almost comical as I look back on it now. If I opened my arms to hug her, Jenna would run right by me, straight to Carole. When I asked if she'd like to have me read her a story, she would take the book and go over to sit in her mommy's lap.

At first, Jenna's rejection of me tore at my heart. This was not a participant in one of my seminars; it was my daughter. My emotions ran the gamut, from self-doubt and frustration to anger and disappointment. I loved her so much and wanted love returned. But the harder I tried, the more she pushed me away.

Gradually I began to understand that, as much as I longed for my daughter's love and approval, I could not force it. So instead of trying to win her affection, I simply sent her love. If she chose to ignore or reject me, I kept my love and support for her continuous and unconditional. Only by letting go of the need for approval can you become unconditional.

Only by letting go of the need for approval can you become unconditional.

My mantra became, "Give her space and send her love." It took considerable discipline and conscious effort at first, but soon I found it more and more comfortable to give Jenna greater freedom about whether or not she chose to connect with me or not. By giving her the space to be herself, I began to enjoy her unique and sparkling spirit even more. And most amazingly, the more I let go of my need for her approval, the more she gave it. She began to rush into my arms the instant she saw me and to crawl up into my lap with a huge stack of books. To this day, whenever we go anywhere, she immediately holds my hand. Our love has grown from conditional and fragile to unconditional and unstoppable.

We all want to be loved. Nothing feels better than the affection and appreciation of those about whom we care deeply. Yet approval and love is something we can happily receive and can't ever force. The instant the need for approval becomes our driving motivation, we become conditional coaches, incapable of the unselfishness, peace of mind, and maturity needed to be our best.

When I signed the letter, "I love you, Brian", I realized that in all the years I had blamed him for my feeling unloved I had never once expressed my love to him.

chapter   twenty   four

Communicating with the Person God Put on the Planet to Test You

Perhaps the most stressful of all communication challenges occurs when you find yourself face-to-face with the person God put on the planet to "test" you!

We all have certain people in our lives with whom we feel so comfortable that we seem to understand one another almost telepathically. We find ourselves blurting out the same thing at precisely the same moment, then laugh together at our spontaneous synchronicity. But with some people, the exact opposite dynamic seems to be at work. If you say "A," they'll say "Z"! It's almost as if you were speaking two completely different languages, entirely devoid of positive emotional connection. The challenge can reach epic proportions when that person is someone with whom you often interact. In some cases, that person is a key teammate in your business, or even your parent, spouse, or child. This is the kind of communication challenge that can create the most disabling stress, draining enormous energy from your spirit.

Discovering a way not only to tolerate one another, but to actually build trust, mutual support, and even affection can become the biggest breakthrough you can achieve as a coach, parent, and communicator. Achieving that breakthrough begins by developing a new understanding of the way human beings relate to one another. All great teachers and coaches recognize that because each individual is different, a personalized approach must be taken to effectively motivate, discipline, teach, and encourage. One of the most important areas of difference to understand as a coach concerns the primary *styles* of communication.

Because each individual is different, a personalized approach must be taken to effectively motivate, discipline, teach, and encourage.

In the communication science known as Neuro Linguistic Programming (NLP) developed by John Grinder and Richard Bandler, we learn that virtually every person has a tendency or preference toward one of three dominant communication styles—either visual, auditory, or kinesthetic.

A visual style is characterized by rapid speech filled with energy, animated physical gesturing, upward eye movement, and the use of sight-oriented words such as *see, picture,* and *examine.* Visual is the rock-n-roll of communication styles. It's the fast-talking, bee-bopping A.M. radio deejay, or the stereotypical salesperson—quick, flamboyant, and exuberant.

The auditory style is the symphony—rich, full, and resonant. Those who favor the auditory style choose phrases like, *I hear what you're saying* or *That sounds great to me.* Their pace is slower and more deliberate, their tone much more melodic and resonant than those who are visual-dominant. The great actor, James Earl Jones (alias

Darth Vader or Mufasa, the Lion King) is a wonderful example of a powerful auditory communicator.

The last of the three dominant communication styles is kinesthetic. With neither the fiery energy and rock-n-roll tempo of the visual style, nor the symphonic balance and richness of the auditory, kinesthetic communication is marked by feeling and heartfelt emotion. It is a softer style, more of touch and tears than of voice and bravado. It is communication you feel rather than show or tell. You transfer your meaning through a hug, a gentle touch, or your emotional presence. Communicators who are kinesthetic-dominant tend to weigh thoughts and feelings carefully, to look down and inward, and to speak more softly than those who favor the other dominant styles.

None of these styles is better than the others. They are simply different. What's more, there is no one who is solely visual, auditory, or kinesthetic. Each of us moves into and out of the three styles at different times. The situation and context in which we find ourselves often determines our style. Yet most of us develop a preference, a dominant style in which we are most comfortable and natural.

The importance and value of this knowledge of communication styles is not derived from using the information as a tool to try to change others, but rather as a key element in changing *ourselves* so we can truly connect at a deeper level. By understanding different communication styles, we can enter another's world and understand his or her feelings and perspective. **As we apply this knowledge we begin to *live* the Golden Rule,**

By understanding different communication styles, we can enter another's world and understand his or her feelings and perspective.

doing unto others as we would have them do unto us. This can create remarkable transformations in our relationship with the people God put on earth to "test" us. In times of stress, using this awareness can free us from a disabling obsession with having to be "right" and on to an enabling determination to work out win-win solutions.

The story of my relationship with my father is a poignant example of the impact the understanding and application of the knowledge of communication styles can have on our lives.

More than anything on earth I wanted him to throw his arms around me and tell me he loved me.

When I was a little boy, my dad was my hero. More than anything on earth I wanted him to throw his arms around me and tell me he loved me. To hear him say, "Brian, you're a great kid!" and to feel him hug me would have meant more to me than any presents anyone could have given. But it was not to be.

My dad had lost his mother at a young age, and with her passing he sealed off a part of his heart so that he would never be as vulnerable again. When he grew up and became a police officer, he kept his feelings carefully in check. He never cried. The only intense emotion I ever saw him show was an occasional flare of anger. To express love and joy through words or physical touch was outside the limits of his reality.

Still, as a young boy I hungered for my father's love. And, just as we develop dominant styles for the way we communicate, we also develop style preferences for the way we give and receive love, respect, and affection.

Though I tend to be a more visual communicator, my dominant style for knowing I'm loved is auditory. I need to hear love expressed to me in words. If someone doesn't say the words *I love you*, the next most powerful way for me to know I'm loved is by feeling it through physical touch (kinesthetic). My dad could simply not express love in either of these ways I so desperately wanted.

The older I became, the more I tried to push away my desire to receive my dad's love and respect. I tried to talk myself out of wanting a close relationship with him. "To heck with him! Who needs him anyway?" I would ask myself over and over again. But he was still my hero in so many ways. Subconsciously I developed an intense inner drive to win his affection. If only I did well enough in school, sports, and leadership—maybe *then* he would come around. Maybe then he would tell me how much he loved me and give me a hug. But he just couldn't do it.

The greatest of all human needs is the need to feel connected.

Just before my eighteenth birthday I went away to college, and for the next fifteen years we had little to do with one another. If I called on the phone and he answered, he'd simply say, "I'll get your mom." I went my way and he went his. I pretended it didn't matter, but that unfulfilled desire for connection with my father never healed. *The greatest of all human needs is the need to feel connected.* The hurt would not go away.

Finally, after years of rationalizing, avoiding, and pretending, I realized how important it was to me to create a real relationship with my father. I decided that I needed to find a way to communicate with him, to open my heart to him and somehow reach in and touch his. I had learned about the three dominant communication styles and knew that I needed to try a different approach if I ever hoped to break down the walls we had erected between us. We had never found a way to really talk with one another face to face or by phone, and I knew he couldn't hug me or connect kinesthetically, so I figured maybe if I wrote him a letter so he could *see* the words, we might begin to break through. For the first time in my life I was determined to communicate completely openly with my father without attempting to force some response or trying to impress him. There was so much I wanted to share with him. I was married to Carole, whom I loved with all my heart, and we had experienced the ultimate of miracles, the birth of our daughter, Kelsey. She was his only grandchild, yet he hardly knew her.

I recognized for the first time how much I have received from my dad and how much I love him.

As soon as I began writing the letter, I was struck with a powerful realization. *I recognized for the first time how much I have received from my dad and how much I love him.* In so many ways, he has become a part of me. I learned about energy from my dad. Much of the time when I was growing up, he worked two jobs so he could earn enough money to take care of us. After working all night as a policeman, he'd pull on his jeans and work another eight hours on construction jobs. He never complained. He was constantly in motion, fixing whatever needed to be fixed, and tackling an endless list of projects. Above all, he taught me to be true to my own word. He had the courage to tell the truth even when he knew his position would be unpopular. The more I wrote, the more I admired my dad.

As I opened my heart to my dad, a second penetrating realization hit me. *I saw clearly for the first time that my dad loved me, too.* He had been expressing his love to me all along. I just didn't get it! My problem was I only knew I was loved when I heard it in words and felt it physically— through the auditory and kinesthetic styles. My dad's sole means of expressing love was *visual,* by taking us places, working extra jobs—by *doing.* He had expressed his love every time he took on a second job. He'd been crying out that he loved me when he had worked for days rebuilding my first bicycle and painting and polishing it until it shined, when he had renovated my room and doubled its size so I could have my own special space, and when he'd driven me all over town for my gazillion extra-curricular activities. Suddenly it became painfully obvious that in all those years I didn't feel he loved me, he had been *showing me* through his actions how much he cared. The love had been there; I simply hadn't seen it!

The love had been there; I simply hadn't seen it!

I finished the letter by thanking my father for all the gifts he had given me that I had been too blind to see. Then I invited him to become a friend to Carole and to discover the incomparable joy of being a grandpa to Kelsey. When I signed the letter, I *love you, Brian,* I realized that in all the years I had blamed him for my feeling unloved I had never once expressed my love to him.

Several weeks after sending off the letter I went out to my mailbox and found an envelope with an address I recognized but handwriting that was unfamiliar. I had never so much as received a postcard from my dad before, so I was stunned to think he had actually written me a letter. I felt my hands trembling as I opened it. Part of me was terribly excited to find out what he had to say, while another part was petrified that I had really angered him and was about to be torn apart.

In the first paragraph, my dad brought me to tears. I felt a kind of happiness and fulfillment I had never experienced before. He began by thanking me for writing my letter. He told me that it must have taken courage to speak so honestly with such a tough old bugger! Then he went on to say how, for as long as he could remember, he had wanted to tell me how much he wished he could be more like me! He had always admired my friendliness and outgoing nature. I couldn't believe this was coming from my dad. I had no idea.

Communication breakthroughs happen when you walk in someone else's shoes and communicate in his or her style.

Then he went on to tell me how proud he was of my various accomplishments in school, as a coach, and in business. I had no clue he even knew about these things, much less cared. He ended by saying how much he wanted to get to know Carole better and to become a real grandfather to Kelsey. When he signed the letter, *Love, Dad*, I felt thirty years of rejection and emptiness instantly evaporate.

This breakthrough with my dad occurred only when I walked in his shoes and communicated with him in his style. It feels so amazing inside to think of my father and smile rather than tighten up in pain. One of the greatest joys in my life is that today, my dad is not only my hero, he is my friend.

The same shining possibility exists for you and those who have been put here to test you. Eagerness to flexibly change your communication style until you find the one that works with each individual you coach is pivotal to building faith, connection, and loyalty among those you serve.

By becoming a dedicated blame-buster you set an example of character, responsibility, and maturity that will make a lasting difference.

chapter   twenty   five

There Is No Blame in the Coaching Hall of Fame!

The breakthrough with my father solidified for me a belief about communication I aspire to live by every day. It is the belief that **the meaning of my communication is the response I generate.** For more than thirty years I had tried to communicate with my father in a way that simply did not work. For most of those years I just kept beating my head against the wall, blaming him for inflexibility and poor communication. Yet nothing changed until I changed *me!*

The first step to the breakthrough was the decision to become a "blame-buster!" If I truly cared, I needed to speak his language, which was *visual.* When I made the choice to step into his shoes and communicate in a way he could receive, it was transformational. The same possibility is alive and available for you.

To become an extraordinary coach and catalyst you must move beyond blame. Blame is the most venomous and insidious destroyer of teams, families, and organizations. It eats at you, sucking your energy and infecting your attitude.

When you think about blame in the context of time, it becomes apparent why blame serves no constructive purpose. Is blame about the past, the present, or the future? From this timeline perspective it becomes immediately obvious that blame is always about the past. Yet you can't undo the past; you can only learn from it. As long as you remain stuck in the emotional quicksand of blame, you stay in the past. Solutions, opportunities, and recovery are available only in the present, creating promise for the future.

Blame is the most venomous and insidious destroyer of teams, families, and organizations.

Moving beyond the past does not mean you pretend nothing ever goes wrong. It simply means that you acknowledge mistakes, take responsibility for your ineffective decisions even if they were well-intended, and then swiftly direct your focus to what you will learn and what you will do next. If you decide it is necessary to discipline the people in your charge, remember your goal, which is to correct and improve. Implement the disciplinary action fairly and calmly. When the consequences have been paid, move forward with a fresh start.

In your interactions with your family, work associates, and friends, if your communication is not generating a positive, productive response, make the decision to become a blame-buster by changing your approach rather than becoming angry and frustrated with them.

Whenever we feel pushed emotionally, we automatically push back. Thus, when blamed, our knee-jerk response is to become defensive. The problem is that we all speak a different language when speaking in defense.

As a blame-buster who accepts the responsibility to change and improve *yourself* when things are not going well, you have an enormous positive impact on your teammates. You create an example that inspires top performances and builds great loyalty. The legendary football coach, Paul "Bear" Bryant of Alabama explained the impact of blame-busting in his down-home country style when he said, "I'm just a country plowhand, but I've learned to get a team beating with one heart: If anything goes great, *they* did it. If anything goes semi-good, *we* did it. If anything goes real bad, *I* did it." When you live by Bryant's sage advice, you'll inspire loyalty rather than back-stabbing, teamwork instead of selfishness.

What feelings and emotions are generated within others—whether teammates, family, friends, or customers—when you sincerely and unselfishly accept responsibility for errors and decisions that did not produce desired results? Instantly others rally around you. Past problems and mistakes have now been accounted for and they are free to let go of the past and move forward to tackle the present and future. Your teammates respect your courage, honesty, and willingness to express your human fallibility. As you demonstrate your humility, you motivate others to seek win-win solutions rather than to waste valuable energy seeking a target for their frustration and fear. The moment you say, "I am responsible. I didn't do a good enough job," "I made a poor decision," or "I did not come through for you," the uncertainty that fuels the upset is over. Then, when you honestly express your commitment to improve

The moment you say, "I am responsible. I didn't do a good enough job," the uncertainty that fuels the upset is over.

your performance, others are ready to refresh their support and optimism.

Full accountability, like real empathy, cannot be contrived or play-acted. Extraordinary coaches thrive on taking responsibility during difficult times because they recognize how it helps remove debilitating guilt and pressure from their teammates. They also realize that accepting full accountability does not mean they must beat themselves up.

Extraordinary coaches thrive on taking responsibility during difficult times because they recognize how it helps remove debilitating guilt and pressure from their teammates.

When you state publicly that your actions have not produced the results you sought, you do not blame yourself. You simply accept the reality that new and different actions are necessary. Your effort and motives may have been well-intended, but change is required to create success. When your new actions create better results, give credit and praise to others without hesitation. Responsibility is something you take, especially during the tough times; credit is something you give whenever you see the opportunity.

A few years ago I had the opportunity to teach a two-and-a-half day seminar for a special group of young people in Fort Worth, Texas. The kids selected for the seminar were high school seniors who had failed to pass a basic competency examination required for graduation in the state of Texas. In fact, these kids had failed the test four times. The maximum number of opportunities students were given to pass the test was five. They were down to their last chance. The exam was scheduled about three weeks after our weekend seminar for the kids.

The program I designed for these young people was aimed at helping them break through negative conditioning, fear, and destructive habits that kept them in the viselike grip of failure. Through games, experiential activities, and stories, my goal was to replace doubt with confidence, indifference with determination. I had taught the course in each of the previous two years with exciting results, so I expected the best. The seminar is vibrant, fun, and activating. Rather than lecturing to the kids, I involve them in experiences that are surprising, thought-provoking, and inspiring.

The easy way out is to give up without even trying.

But as I began to work with this particular group, I could see I was in for a major challenge. It was immediately apparent to me that these kids were bright enough to pass the test. They were creative, quick-thinking, and energetic—as long as they weren't in the classroom. As soon as they were asked to be attentive and to learn, however, they shut down. At first, I thought they just didn't care. But then I began to see they were simply afraid. Subconsciously they had resigned themselves to failure. The easy way out was to give up without even trying. They could then slough the whole thing off with a convenient rationalization: "I could have passed the test if I wanted to. It just wasn't any big deal."

The more I tried to involve the kids and build enthusiasm, the more they pushed back. They didn't do so by being aggressive, but rather by mentally checking out. Not once in hundreds of seminars had I encountered a group so disconnected and unmotivated. The physical participation, fun, and heart in the program had always won over even the most skeptical teams. But these kids were yawning, falling asleep, and paying zero attention.

As I struggled through the first day, I began to get frustrated with the kids despite my best intentions. Luckily, just as my frustration was starting to escalate into anger, I arrived at the section in the seminar that focused on blame-busting, and I remembered that the meaning of my communication is the response I generate. I decided to take a risk.

The meaning of your communication is the response you generate.

When we finished a game that is designed to point out the futility of blame, I stepped forward and got right in the kids faces. They had sleep-walked through the game with their typical indifference. Up until this point I had met every yawn with patience and kindness. But now, in a stern, almost menacing voice I stared icily into each of their eyes and said, "You know, I came 2,000 miles, spending four days away from my wife and children to be here with you. And you're not getting a thing from it."

As I scolded the kids I watched their reaction closely. It was exactly what I had hoped for. A couple of them nudged one another and gave just a hint of a triumphant smile as if to say, "We're getting to him. He's losing it." They *wanted* me to give up on them and leave them alone. Then they would have an airtight excuse to give up on themselves. They could just mess around for the rest of the time and pin the worthlessness of the seminar on the teacher who lost his cool.

Encouraged by their response, I became even more intense. I said, "It would be so easy for me right now to say—what's *wrong* with you!" Once again I could sense the growing feeling among the kids that I had indeed lost it and would soon be out of their hair.

But what I said next shocked them. "It would be so easy for me to blame you for not caring about anything important. *But if I did that, I'd be dead wrong!*"

Several of the kids did double-takes and looked at me as if to ask, "Huh? What did he say?"

Impassioned, I went on, "There are ideas, principles, and possibilities in this class that can do more than help you pass that test in three weeks so you can walk across the stage on graduation day. There is value here that can change your life! But you're not getting it because I haven't been a good enough teacher to help you see. If I blamed you I'd be dead wrong. If you're not finding the value that's right here today, I've got to change *me*!"

If you're not getting it, it's because I haven't been a good enough teacher to help you see.

For the first time in our more than six hours together every eye in the room was glued to me. They weren't used to having someone take responsibility for their attitudes and indifference. They were used to being blamed. Suddenly they were confused, but interested and attentive.

I next told them a story about one of my dearest friends who broke free from addiction to cocaine through the unconditional love and support of an intervention team. It is an intense, emotional story I rarely tell in my seminars. I had not planned to share the story with the kids, but right at that moment my intuition told me it was the right thing to do. As I told the story you could have heard a pin drop in the room. Every one of those kids was right with me, hanging on every word. I saw several of them choke up with emotion. I realized that here was a story with which they could identify. They have seen more drugs, violence, and fear in their seventeen or eighteen years than most people see in a lifetime. When I finished telling the story, something happened I will never forget. One by one those kids stood up and gave me a standing ovation. Ten minutes earlier I was on the verge of losing them. Had I chosen blame, I surely would have. Later, each of the students broke a one-inch thick wooden board karate-style as a personal metaphor for breaking through. On the front of the board they wrote about a fear, habit, or obstacle they were determined to move beyond in their lives. On the other side of the board they described the feelings, accomplishments, and positive changes they would create for themselves and those they loved when they successfully broke through. The support and energy in the room during board breaking flew right off the charts!

About two months later I received a letter from one of the kids telling me that she and several others had passed the test. She wrote, "When we were taking the test we brought along our broken boards. Now we are ready to graduate in May. Even the ones that didn't pass made improvement. We are very thankful to you for encouraging us to think positive and to believe in ourselves.

As coaches and leaders, we do not control other people, we only affect them through our vision, actions and example.

Without you pushing us on, I don't think we would have made it. Thank you, Tanesha."

As coaches and leaders, it is important to remember that we do not control other people, we only affect them through our vision, actions, and example. The only person we directly control is the one we see in the mirror. By becoming a dedicated blame-buster you set an example of character, responsibility, and maturity that will make a lasting difference.

Strive to be fully present for those you love in every precious moment!

chapter   twenty   six

Change the Ratio – Change Your World!

A few years ago, Daryl Kollman, a noted educator, researcher, and speaker coined the phrase, *Change the ratio and change the world.* The ratio he referred to was the pro-portion of criticism to praise. Studies have shown that the norm in our culture is thirty-five criticisms for every one statement of praise. Though criticisms are often disguised as sarcasm and teasing they still send potent messages to the subconscious. We have developed a collective fixation on what we don't want, don't like, or don't respect.

In the field of personal development, a long-standing principle states: "What we focus on is what we get." I believe the principle needs some updating. Particularly when it comes to coaching, parenting, and leading, what we focus on is what we *create.* When we direct thirty-five times more attention towards criticism than praise, is it any wonder we constantly create more to criticize?

Imagine a five-year-old boy with a brand new, two-wheeler bicycle. Until now, he had always ridden a tricycle or a bike with training wheels. But today he's going for it. As he sets off down the sidewalk (with his tongue hanging out the side of his mouth for balance) he's concentrating with all his might. The bike is tilting and wobbling like crazy as he pedals forward. But, despite his shakiness, he's actually riding! Suddenly, right in the middle of the side-walk, thirty-feet in front of him, is a great big rock! What does he do? You've got it. With his eyes super-glued to the rock he teeters himself smack into it, like a missile locked onto its target. *Bam!* He hits the rock and crashes in a heap. He struggles back to his feet, walks by his dad with-out a whimper, and then spots his mom. Instantly he bursts into tears as she wraps her arms around him.

The Pygmalion effect explains that our expectations and beliefs create a magnetlike attraction in the direction of those thoughts.

Now it's two weeks later. Same boy, same bike, same sidewalk—bigger rock! But now he's cool and confident. He has this bike riding thing down pat! As he pedals for-ward now, what happens? Right! Just as he approaches the rock, he deftly and effortlessly steers himself around it— unless, of course, he jumps it!

The key question to ask about this story is, "What goes around the rock first?" Before his front wheel sped around the obstacle, *his eyes envisioned the way.* What he focused on was what he created.

The same is true when you change the ratio of criti-cism to praise in your communication. One of the most important coaching principles, dubbed the Pygmalion effect, explains that our expectations and beliefs create a magnetlike attraction in the direction of those thoughts. You create the Pygmalion effect for others through your words, voice qualities, and body language. We are always Pygmalions to one another, sending subconscious messages in concert with our beliefs and expectations. The only question is what kind. Positive, negative, or neutral? When you change your personal ratio away from criticism and toward praise, you instantly become a *positive* Pygmalion, directing your creative attention to the possibility, potential, and strength in yourself and those around you.

Recently I found myself being excessively critical of my oldest daughter, Kelsey. I was on her constantly, chiding her to be more responsible. Even when helping with her schoolwork, I snapped at her impatiently when she didn't check her math problems more carefully or misspelled words I felt she should know. The more I rode her, the more mistakes she made. If only I would have opened my eyes, I could have seen how I was hurting her confidence and stifling her spirit. The crazy part was, I am extremely upbeat and positive with virtually everyone I know. But with my own precious daughter I had slipped into a ratio of criticism to praise that was destructive rather than reflective of the love and admiration I truly felt for her. Had I continued on this path I could have done irreparable harm to our relationship and her belief in herself.

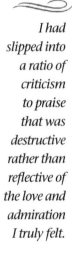

I had slipped into a ratio of criticism to praise that was destructive rather than reflective of the love and admiration I truly felt.

I will be forever thankful to a dear friend who e-mailed me a classic story about fatherhood just at that crucial time. The story shook me to my core. He had no idea how perfect his timing was, and how much his thoughtfulness in sending the e-mail continues to affect me and my family every single day. The story was written long ago by

W. Livingston Larned, and when I received it that evening, I sat down and adapted Larned's masterpiece into a letter that now hangs above my desk as a daily reminder of my commitment as a father, coach, friend, and human being.

FATHER FORGETS
Adapted from W. Livingston Larned

What has habit been doing to me? The habit of finding fault, of reprimanding —this was my reward to you for being a child.

Listen, Kelsey and Jenna: I am saying this as you lie asleep, one little paw crumpled under your cheek and the brown curls stickily wet on your damp forehead. I have stolen into your room alone. Just a few minutes ago, as I sat reading in my office, a stifling wave of remorse swept over me. Guiltily I came to your bedside.

These are the things I was thinking, precious ones: I had been cross to you. I scolded you as you were dressing for school because you gave your face merely a dab with a towel. I took you to task for not cleaning your room. I called out angrily when you threw some of your things on the floor.

At breakfast I found fault, too. You spilled things. You ate so little of your food. You put your elbows on the table. You spread butter too thick on your bread. And as you turned and waved a hand and called, "Good-bye, Daddy!" I frowned, and said in reply, "Are you ever going to learn to stand up straight!"

Then it began all over again in the late afternoon. As I came up the road I spied you, down on your knees,

playing Barbies. There were holes in your socks. I humiliated you before your friends by marching you ahead of
me to your room. Stockings were expensive—and if you
had to buy them you would be more careful! Imagine
that, my beauties, from a father!

Do you remember, later, when I was reading, how you
came in timidly, with a sort of hurt look in your eyes?
When I glanced up over my paper, impatient at the inter-
ruption, you hesitated at the door. "What is it you want?"
I snapped.

It was not that I did not love you; it was that I expected too much of youth.

You said nothing, but ran across in one tempestuous
plunge, and threw your arms around my neck and kissed
me, and your small arms tightened with an affection that
God had sent blooming in your heart and which even
neglect could not wither. And then you were gone, pat-
tering up the stairs.

Well, my daughters, it was shortly afterward that my
paper slipped from my hands and a terrible sickening fear
came over me. What has habit been doing to me? The
habit of finding fault, of reprimanding—this was my
reward to you for being a child. It was not that I did not
love you; it was that I expected too much of youth. I was
measuring you by the yardstick of my own years.

And there was so much that was good and fine and
true in your character. The little heart of you was as big as
the dawn itself over the wide hills. This was shown by
your spontaneous impulse to rush in and kiss me good
night. Nothing else matters tonight, girls. I have come to
your bedside in the darkness, and I have knelt there,

ashamed!

It is a feeble atonement: I know you would not understand these things if I told them to you during your waking hours. But tomorrow I will be a real daddy! I will chum with you, and suffer when you suffer, and laugh when you laugh. I will bite my tongue when impatient words come. I will keep saying as if it were a ritual: "She is just a little girl—a precious, loving little girl!"

Instead of condemning people, let's try to understand them.

I am afraid I have visualized you as grown women. Yet as I see you now, my darlings, crumpled and weary in your beds, I see that you are still children. Yesterday you were in your mother's arms, your head on her shoulder. I have asked too much, too much.

Instead of condemning people, let's try to understand them. Let's try to figure out why they do what they do. That's a lot more profitable and intriguing than criticism; and it breeds sympathy, tolerance and kindness. "To know all is to forgive all."

As Dr. Johnson said: "God himself, sir, does not propose to judge man until the end of his days."

Why should you and I?

My Incredible Girls—I shall strive to be fully present for you in every precious moment!

I love you, Daddy

Today, begin communicating the ability and resourcefulness you see in others, especially when their results are not yet matching their efforts. It is the most effectual ongoing action you can take to help bring out their best and one that will come naturally to you as you adjust your focus to look through the eyes of a coach.

No matter what great things you accomplish, somebody helps you.

chapter twenty seven

World-Class Buddy Thanking! Transforming Your Team Through the Power of Simple Appreciation

A great strategy for changing the ratio of criticism to praise is to become a "world-class buddy thanker." When you live with an attitude of gratitude, it becomes natural to catch others doing things right. But let me ask you an eye-opening question. Who are the people in our lives we tend to forget to thank the most?

I've asked this question in every seminar I've ever taught, and have always heard similar responses. The people we most often forget to thank are those to whom we are the closest—our spouse, children, parents, or the people we work beside everyday. When triggered by the question we see how easily we can fall into the habit of taking the people we love most for granted. We can rationalize that we don't need to tell the prized people in our lives know how we feel about them because they should already know, but the end result of neglect is decay and diminution. The more we fall into the habit of taking others for granted and withholding our appreciation, the more disconnected we become from the countless blessings in our lives.

Have you ever looked up into a brilliant blue sky and spotted a brightly colored hot-air balloon floating on the breeze? Once when I stood enjoying such a scene, the thought struck me that fresh, exciting relationships are like those beautiful balloons. They are light, vibrant, and colorful. Filled with energy, they soar effortlessly. They are lighter than air! That's just the way we feel when we fall in love, welcome our children into the world, join a new team, or make a new friend. It feels so easy and natural to thank our buddies when we're in the "glow."

Fresh, exciting relationships are like beautiful hot-air balloons– light, vibrant and colorful.

But what happens when we begin to take them for granted? As I pictured the balloon it occurred to me that the first time we forget to express our thanks, it's as if we take an acupuncture needle and pierce the balloon. Acupuncture needles are so skinny, the small puncture wouldn't cause the balloon to explode all at once. Yet the instant the needle pierces the balloon, you start a slow leak. Each succeeding time you forget to thank your buddy and take him or her more for granted, it's as if you stick another needle in the balloon, and then another, and another, until eventually enough of the small leaks accumulate, and the balloon begins to fall. As it drops out of the sky, it will look as if the color fades away. With our relationships it will feel as if the spark has begun to fade. Where there was once spirit, energy, and connection, there will be emptiness and detached coexistence.

How do you reverse this downward cycle and keep your relationships alive and energized? The answer is found in an important coaching strategy: the principle of *exaggeration*. A simple example will make this principle crystal clear.

When I was a swimming coach, a common technique flaw that many of the kids needed to overcome in the freestyle stroke (or crawl) was the habit of not pulling far enough under the center of their body where they had the greatest leverage and power. But if I attempted to correct swimmers who had developed a wide arm pull by saying, "Pull down the centerline of your body," what do you think they said to me in response?

Looking at me as if I had lost my marbles, they'd reply in exasperation, "I am!" As a coach it is crucial to remember that what you see may not match what your protégés are feeling. These kids had become comfortable pulling wide under their bodies. The feeling was ingrained as a habit. They already thought they were performing correctly.

You can apply the principle of exaggeration to invigorate your relationships by becoming a world-class-buddy thanker.

That meant it did absolutely no good to tell them how to do it. What did I need to do to help them make the desired change? I had to apply the principle of exaggeration. I instructed them to pull as far across their body underwater as they could so the right hand swept way left under their bodies, and the left hand crossed way over to the right. As soon as they attempted to follow these instructions, guess where they pulled? Zap! Their pull came right down under the centerline of the body!

As they exaggerated in this way, how do you think it felt? At first, it was strange and uncomfortable. But the more they stayed with it, the more natural the motion became. Soon they settled into the new habit.

Taking those we love for granted is nothing more than a habit. You can apply the principle of exaggeration to invigorate your relationships by becoming a world-class-buddy thanker just as the swimmers applied the principle to improve their strokes. Write personal cards to friends, teammates, and family members expressing your gratitude and admiration even when it's not their birthday or anniversary. These "happy, heck-of-it" cards will delight the recipients, and they will once again know they are important. E-mail and voice mail provide fantastic opportunities to give compliments and to say thanks. Create "moments" for the special people in your life by giving unexpected gifts, arranging surprise events, or simply taking the time to be fully present as you tell them how much you appreciate them.

Make it a regular habit to ask yourself, "What am I truly grateful for right now?"

As a coach, the example you set as a world-class buddy thanker will stimulate great support within your team. In all the studies undertaken to examine the effects of recognition and acknowledgment, not one has found a business, team, or family that had too much! Make it a regular habit to ask yourself, "What am I truly grateful for right now?" Instantly, you'll remember an important truth that will both humble and inspire you. As Olympic champion Wilma Rudolph expressed so perfectly, "No matter what great things you accomplish, somebody always helps you."

The more I let go and gave them the ball, the more they had to think, integrate, and stretch. And so did I!

chapter twenty eight

Let Go, Let Grow

Of all the strategies and principles we've explored in this book to give you a coaching edge, the most difficult one for me to adopt personally has been *letting* go. As a father, every time my daughters come to me for help with school projects, and as a speaker and teacher, every time I encounter hard skeptics who choose to push away ideas I *know* could elevate the quality of their lives, I must discipline myself to let go.

This is a tough one for an emotional person like me, because I care deeply about the people I serve, and I want to take great care of them to be sure they're protected and safe. With my family, those feelings are even stronger. All too often, though, that concern leads to the desire to control others rather than to help them grow.

Every year I conduct a one week-long train-the-trainer program where I certify trainers and speakers to teach the seminars I've designed. As I prepared for the first class in this program, I began to realize what an enormous amount of information the participants would need to absorb before they would be ready to present my seminars with confidence and passion. There was so much to learn and so many nuances to master. The more I prepared, the more determined I became to give the participants the most complete, comprehensive, and exciting training experience they could imagine.

When the participants arrived, I was pumped. That first group was highly motivated and extremely talented. Most of them already had considerable speaking and training experience. Their excitement was evident as we dove right into the material.

*It doesn't matter how much **you know**—what really matters is how much **they learn.***

There was only one problem. In all my preparation, I had completely forgotten the importance of letting go. Instead, I had set out to teach them everything I knew. I was going to cram every bit of information I had learned over the years into them in this five-day course.

By the time we took our first break I could sense something wasn't quite right. These intelligent, highly capable people, who'd started out completely inspired, were beginning to look like zombies. They reminded me of Rocky Balboa, sitting on his stool in the corner trying to shake the cobwebs out of his rattled brain after having absorbed unbelievable punishment in the first round. Their eyes were glazed, they were already overloaded, and we still had four-and-a-half days to go!

Unfortunately, instead of remembering one of my most fundamental coaching philosophies—if it's not working, try something different—I just kept hammering them with more and more information. The only change I made was in my own intensity. I did not let go—I held on tighter. It took me two days before I realized I was doing all the talking.

They made it through the course thanks to their remarkable endurance, but I knew I had fallen far short of adequately preparing them to teach my seminars. They had more than enough talent to excel, they had simply not been given the chance to test their wings. I never worked so hard in my life and accomplished so little. I had tried to carry them on my shoulders instead of letting them run.

By letting go of the need to control, you are able to be far more alert and present.

Luckily, I took the time to integrate what I had learned from that first experience and finally saw how different the training would have been for the participants had I remembered to let go.

In the second and subsequent train-the-trainer programs, I disciplined myself to talk about seventy-five percent less, and instead had the participants carry the ball. I designed the course to flow in bite-sized chunks. Each segment began with a brief, concise overview. Then I teamed them up in pairs to practice, practice, practice! Immediately they were in the game instead of on the sidelines. Their energy soared, and I was amazed at how rapidly they mastered the material. From day one of the class I remembered to ask more than tell. We not only covered far more ground than in the first program, we easily moved beyond memorizing information into exciting areas such as their presentation skills, presence, and how to integrate the training into every aspect of their lives. They left confident, motivated, and prepared to go out and make a difference. By letting go, I had indeed let them grow.

As I look back now, the most surprising result of letting go was that it caused *me* to grow far more, as well. Instead of spouting information, I became a real coach. I began to see it didn't matter how much *I* knew—what really mattered was what they *learned.* As they took ownership of the material, they became real artists instead of technicians painting by the numbers. The more I let go and gave them the ball, the more they had to think, integrate, and stretch. And so did I! By letting go of the need to control, I was able to be far more alert and present. As a result, the class was infinitely more fun, spontaneous, and on-target for each participant. What's more, I came up with dozens of brand new ideas and insights I've introduced into subsequent seminars that have made them even more impactful. For the first time I understood that letting go is a win-win strategy.

As a coach, your goal is to have your teammates stand on their own two feet as confident, energetic, and positive leaders.

As a coach of any kind, your foremost goal is to have your teammates stand on their own two feet as confident, energetic, and positive leaders. You want them to enjoy making decisions and not be shackled by the fear of failure. No matter how much you care, somewhere along the line you must give them the ball for this vision to become reality. You must let go of your need to control them without ever letting go of your unconditional love and support. When you do, you send an unmistakable message that you believe in them. Bolstered by that confidence and trust, they will grow as never before.

You must follow through and do what you say to create lasting positive change whether in your business, your family, or your community.

chapter twenty nine

Care, Dare, and Make Aware: How to Ensure Dynamic Communication

In the past several years the business world has seen many companies, from high-tech industries to network marketing, experience phenomenal growth. In many cases that explosive growth created intense challenges with employees, structures, and systems stretched to unheard-of extremes practically overnight. For example, in some companies, customer service and order lines became completely clogged during these times of hyper-growth. Customers' loyalty and patience were severely tested by long waiting times, slow service, and backorders resulting from supply that couldn't keep pace with demand. What's more, employee stress and competitive pressure seemed to intensify each day during these challenging times.

Yet some of these organizations not only survived, they emerged more successful than ever. How did they do it? They found the answer through the same combination of on-target communication and aggressive strategic action that will create dynamic results in your family just as in your business. It's crucial to remember that communication without subsequent action will, at best, temporarily ease pressure. You must follow through and do what you say to create lasting positive change whether in your business, your family, or your community.

Backed up with that commitment to action, on-target communication in stressful times requires three critical elements:

1. Empathy

2. Full Accountability

3. Progressive Information

You can immerse yourself in another perspective when you express genuine empathy.

As a coach, you can effectively mesh these three to ease tension, build understanding, and renew faith. Let's look at each of these three keys.

Empathy: Real empathy is the result of truly stepping into others' shoes. It requires listening and an open mind. It is never contrived nor phony, because you can immerse yourself in another perspective when you express genuine empathy.

For example, a few years ago I consulted extensively with an organization during their rapid growth period. At that time their distributors were experiencing frustrating telephone waiting times and busy signals. Several of the most distressed callers were referred to me. Whenever I communicated with these disgruntled distributors, my voice was filled with empathy. These were good people about whom I cared deeply, and I felt their frustration, concern, and stress. Their time was important, and their upset understandable. By genuinely stepping into their shoes, they knew someone cared. My empathy increased their patience and positive solution-orientation. As a result, we were able to work out even the toughest challenges.

Full Accountability: Few elements of communication are more powerful—and more rare—than full accountability. When you are fully accountable, you accept total responsibility for your words and actions. You live by the belief you read earlier: The meaning of my communication is the response I generate. Automatically, you become a dedicated blame-buster. Instead of making excuses, you step up to the plate and shoulder the responsibility for challenges, errors, and mistakes.

When you are fully accountable, you accept total responsibility for your words and actions.

Progressive Information: Once others sense your genuine empathy and recognize your determination to accept full accountability during times of stress, you must supply them with the facts: actions and strategies for moving the team in the direction of its goals and vision. This *progressive information* must be solid, concrete, and verifiable. Deliver progressive information without embellishment. You simply state the facts and the benefits derived from those actions. Describing the benefits answers the central question on the minds of those you coach: "How will this affect me?" Through progressive information you help transform detachment into personal involvement.

Occasionally you can increase the impact of progressive information by providing a relative perspective so your team can more fully grasp the improvement and changes being made. You want to deliver a "snapshot shock" by using a "before and after" context. This strategy gains its strength from our tendency to become desensitized to changes unless we are suddenly presented with dramatic comparison. Snapshot shock is like time-lapse photography. Small, almost imperceptible incremental changes add up over time to create remarkable transformations.

When you provide progressive information during times of stress you create the snapshot shock reaction. Instead of taking things for granted, the improvement is recognized and appreciated much more fully. When you help others experience a "snapshot shock" as they evaluate their own progress, it can immediately set them back on a positive track. They may not have noticed how far they'd come. Once again, the result of applying this key to on-target communication is deepened faith and trust in themselves and their team.

Instead of taking things for granted, the improvement is recognized and appreciated much more fully.

These three elements can be summarized as care, dare, and make aware. *Care* enough to demonstrate true empathy; *dare* to take responsibility for obstacles, challenges, and mistakes; and, *make others fully aware* of the genuine progress that is being made. It is a truly winning coaching combination guaranteed to elevate the effectiveness of your communication during stressful times to a new level.

Foundations of Effective Communication During Times of Stress

- *Keep your communication flowing when the going gets tough.*

- *Inject humor in your communication to help break negative patterns.*

- *View your communication as a <u>series</u> using three key tools: Become a master of <u>metaphor:</u> stories open doors, lectures close them! <u>Summarization</u> dramatically increases retention. <u>Enabling Questions</u> are far more important to quality communication than answers.*

- *Use your understanding of communication styles—visual, auditory, and kinesthetic—to step into others' shoes and truly connect.*

- *Reverse the normal ratio of criticism to praise (remember thirty-five to one) in your communication and watch your business—and your life—soar!*

- *<u>Care, dare, and make aware</u>—become a master of these three crucial elements in transformational communication— empathy, responsibility, and progressive information to lift your team to new heights, even during the toughest times!*

Recognize and acknowledge examples of breakthrough thinking and actions. The past does not have to equal the future.

chapter thirty

The Past Is Not Your Future

As a coach, one of the most important beliefs to keep constantly in mind is that *the past does not have to equal the future.* This principle is a must for possibility-oriented teams. It seems a logical and simple enough thought intellectually, yet it is most severely tested during times of stress. One of your most important challenges as a coach is to instill this foundational belief emotionally into the heart of every team member, beginning with your own heart.

When you stop to think about it, every major breakthrough is the result of the future being different from the past. Yet many of us fear and fight change because we build an almost air-tight comfort zone, even when the results we are generating from our current habits are falling far short of our goals. The belief that the future doesn't have to be a rerun of the past helps us remember that we've been given the ultimate gift—a brand new now. It refreshes our spirit and adds fuel to our possibilities.

In my seminars, as we prepare for board breaking I tell a story that reveals the potential we can discover when we open to the belief that the future can be completely different from the past. It is a story about a remarkable test of human spirit that is held annually Down Under.

For many years a running race known as the "King of the Ultra-marathons" has been held in Australia. An ultra-marathon is any race *longer* than marathon distance, from twenty-seven miles on up. I had read in awe about races as long as one hundred miles and the almost super-human endurance and determination of the few elite runners who tackle such enormous challenges, but nearly fell off my chair when I learned that the King of the Ultras covers six hundred kilometers! That is just about 375 miles.

Every major breakthrough is the result of the future being different from the past.

The athletes who competed in the King were the finest extreme-endurance runners in the world. As you would imagine, they were extraordinary physical specimens. They were rail-thin with practically zero excess body-fat. Their legs looked like the drawings of pure muscle fiber found in physiology text books, and they wore the lightest, most efficiently designed running shoes and clothing money could buy. Their ages ranged from early twenties to mid-thirties. That was the name of the game until the year Cliff Young showed up.

When Cliff first arrived for the race, he was the object of immediate curiosity. First of all, no one had ever seen him at any other ultra-races. What's more, though he was fit, he looked older than the other runners and wasn't dressed in the expensive, high-quality gear used by the elite competitors. In fact, he wore baggy shorts, and his shoes looked something like old-fashioned high-top sneakers. A race official eventually approached Cliff to find out what he was doing there.

Cliff answered in his rich Aussie accent, "Me nime is Cliff Young, and I come to run the rice."

The official replied, "Well, Mr. Young, I've been around ultra-racing for many years, and I've never seen you at any events before. Where have you competed in the past?"

Cliff's response nearly floored the official. "Well, actually, I've never run a rice befo'. I jist thought I'd entah this one!"

The official didn't know whether to laugh or have Cliff escorted away, but recovered enough from his shock to finally ask, "What makes you possibly think you can run a six hundred–kilometer race?"

Cliff looked at the man with great earnestness and explained, "Me whole life I've lived and worked on a sheep station in the Outback. And I never 'ad a horse. I've been running after bloody sheep so far and so long, when I heard of your rice, I thought to meself, 'Cliffy, why not give 'er a go for the prize money?' "

The official didn't know what to make of a character like Cliff and just smiled, shook his head, and walked away, thinking to himself, *Well, he's loony but at least he's harmless.*

Then Cliff began to warm up. A few people spied him in his baggy shorts and heavy-looking shoes and could hardly keep from laughing. Not only was he dressed

We've been given the ultimate gift–a brand new now.

strangely, he didn't run like a runner. With arms hanging limply by his sides and his feet shuffling along, he ran like a *noodle*. Those watching him probably thought about calling the paramedics. He didn't look like he could run six minutes much less six hundred kilometers!

Up to that time, according to past wisdom, the only way for a human being to stand the extreme physical, mental, and emotional stress of this mind-boggling race was to run no more than twelve to fourteen hours in each twenty-four hour period. The race lasted several days. The belief was that if you didn't give yourself at least twelve hours of rest each day, you would break down and be unable to finish. The elite runners all ran according to this formula, running three to six hour chunks and then taking a few hours to eat, refuel, rest, and recover.

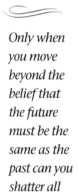

Only when you move beyond the belief that the future must be the same as the past can you shatter all previous limits.

But no one told Cliff. More important, no one had ever told the sheep! Out on the sheep station, if Cliff decided to take a rest for several hours those woollies were gone! So he learned a different style out of necessity.

In the first twenty-four hours, Cliff just kept noodling along. Then he rested for a short while, grabbed a quick bite and went right back at it. To make a long story short, not only did Cliff win the race, he broke the world record by a day and a half! The best part is that when Cliff pulled off this astonishing accomplishment he was sixty-one years old!

Cliff didn't know the past, so he created an entirely new approach that shocked everyone. One year later, four different people broke Cliff's record. How did they do it?

You guessed it—they noodled! It turned out that Cliff's funny looking running style was the most efficient way to cover such extraordinary distances because he used so little antagonistic force. He didn't work against himself, and like the fuel-saving cars developed because of the gas and oil shortage of the seventies, he simply ran more efficiently. The next year, several of the top runners modeled key aspects of Cliff's style and ran better than one-and-a-half days faster than they'd ever done before. Only when you move beyond the belief that the future must be the same as the past can you shatter all previous limits.

Fear holds us in the past. You job as a coach is to break through that fear and set spirits free.

You build this belief into your team by making it a point to recognize and acknowledge examples of break-through thinking and actions. In business, when you see one of your teammates step beyond past habits and try a new approach that enhances service, teamwork, or performance be sure to share that success story with others on the team. In your family, when your children show improvement in areas in which they had previously struggled, let them know how terrific they are and how much you admire their courage and perseverance. Create an atmosphere wherever you coach that encourages fresh approaches and well-intentioned risk-taking—even when those new actions don't produce improved results. Fear holds us in the past. Your job as a coach is to break through that fear and set spirits free. Remember, whatever has taken us to where we are now, is probably not going to be all it takes to move to the next level. Only when we change do we grow.

chapter   thirty   one

Failing to Prepare is Preparing to Fail!

When you look for a common denominator shared by outstanding coaches in all fields, one emerges as an absolute requirement for excellence. Personalities, styles, and methods of great coaches vary dramatically, but commitment to *preparation* is a fundamental they all can agree is crucial.

Most often we think of preparation in terms of conditioning and strategic planning. Both of these aspects of preparation are important ingredients in quality coaching. Conditioning demands repetition physically, emotionally, and mentally to the point where desired actions become automatic and natural. Great coaches build enthusiasm and commitment about mastering fundamentals through repetition.

Strategic planning is the aspect of mental preparation that aims at anticipating future events and positioning your team for opportunities and competitive advantages. Coaches who excel in strategic planning study their own team's strengths and weaknesses as well as their competition's tendencies and strategies. Then they use that information and intelligence to focus the direction of their conditioning.

Three key areas are most important when it comes to preparing your team, whether your primary coaching focus is in business, athletics, education, or family. These three are also the areas most vital to preparing yourself. The first is preparing the *spirit.*

Preparing the spirit: In the movie *Apollo 13*, there's an unforgettable scene where a team of NASA scientists and technicians is handed a nonsensical collection of odd-shaped replicas of the spacecraft's internal air filter system parts. They have less than twelve hours to figure out how to get the model up and running so they can instruct the astronauts in fixing their own system. The technical ground crew knows that if they fail, the astronauts will die of suffocation.

Great coaches build enthusiasm and commitment about mastering fundamentals through repetition.

Had that same challenge been presented to them as a practice assignment without the urgency of life and death attached, it would have been easy for them to give up when an answer seemed out of reach. But with the world watching and real lives on the line, that team absolutely refused to fail. They would do whatever it took to find a solution in time to save the astronauts. For eleven and a half hours, thoughts of fatigue, hunger, or doubt simply did not exist. There had to be a way. Their unstoppable energy and focus won!

That group of technicians was a team with a *compelling why*—a purpose that ignited their tireless energy and laser focus so they were able to perform at their best. As a coach, the most important element in preparing the spirit is to help those around you discover their compelling whys. For some, the compelling why centers around service to others and making a significant difference. For others, it is the challenge itself which inspires maximum commitment and energy. Still others are driven by the desire for recognition. Your job as coach is to connect these individual compelling whys into an energized, collective purpose.

The single greatest tool you possess to help those you coach beat with one heart is consistent and determined emphasis on the value of teamwork. Reward unselfish actions and behind-the-scenes contributions that are easily overlooked by those who have not yet learned to see through the eyes of a coach. Make the decision to plan events that are one hundred percent focused on building team spirit and enthusiasm. It is an investment that pays enormous long-term dividends; when those you coach feel a part of something bigger than themselves, they know they are important and that they make a difference to others who depend upon them for their unique contributions. A team with a well-prepared spirit fully understands that it's amazing what's accomplished when no one cares who gets the credit—and everyone loves to give it!

The most important element in preparing the spirit is to help those around you discover their compelling whys.

Preparing the mind: The most important coaching secret when it comes to preparing the mind is to ingrain a truly constructive belief system about adversity.

I always marveled at the legendary Swedish tennis star

Bjorn Borg and his amazing coolness under pressure. He seemed to kick into an entirely different gear on those rare occasions when he found himself falling behind in a match. For most of us, adversity seems to gain momentum from itself like a train hurtling out of control, but Borg had the uncanny ability to reverse the negative force in an instant.

He revealed his secret in an interview after he had fought back from two sets down to win yet another Wimbeldon Championship. He told the reporter that he had long observed how most players tightened up when things began to go against them and their shots started missing. They responded to the adversity in one of two ways. Some players became frustrated and angry and their game caved in. After a few attempts at smacking the ball as hard as they could and watching it fly out of the court, they simply gave up. They tried to use negative force instead of positive power. They felt cheated and unfairly treated. Others tried to back off and place their shots, sacrificing power for improved accuracy. They just tried to keep the ball in play and hoped their opponents cooled off and began to make some errors.

If he found himself being outplayed, he challenged himself to take more chances.

Borg saw that neither of these strategies created much hope for success, so he developed an unusual approach. If he found himself being outplayed, he challenged himself to take more chances. He went for the lines and added power to his strokes. Most important, he let go of any worry about the other player and simply zeroed in on his own play. This was pivotal, because though he increased his power and hit the ball harder, he did so with *positive* focus rather than with resigned fatalism. The more he intensified his concentration, the more fun he had.

The results of his calculated risk taking were extraordinary. When players are on fire, they often talk about how they seem to see the ball all the way to the racquet strings—the tennis moment of truth. In preparing himself to respond to adversity by becoming more pro-active and aggressive, he automatically increased his concentration on the point of contact with the ball, and his shots began to land with greater pace and accuracy. Suddenly, his confidence soared. At the same time, his opponent began to press. Borg's upward spiral was amplified by the acceleration of his opponent's downward spiral. The next thing you knew, there was the quiet Swede, arms raised in triumph, while on the other side of the net stood a confused, deflated runner-up trying to understand how the match got away.

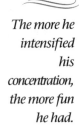

The more he intensified his concentration, the more fun he had.

You can prepare your children to deal with adversity with the same kind of positive energy as exemplified by Borg. A recent winner of the Nobel Prize renowned for the extraordinary creativity he brought to the study of physics was asked about the biggest influences on his life. Without hesitation he spoke about his mother and her unusual way of dealing with mistakes and adversity.

He told of one incident when, as a young boy, he had sneaked downstairs and gulped down some milk right out of the carton. As he reached up to the top shelf to put the carton back, he spotted his mother out of the corner of his eye, standing quietly in the kitchen doorway watching him. Startled, he lost his grip on the heavy carton. It crashed to the floor and broke open. Milk spilled everywhere.

Most parents, having caught their son red-handed doing something forbidden, would have responded with anger and frustration. If the boy compounded his naughtiness by making such a horrible mess, the angry response would in all likelihood intensify.

Through the eyes of a coach you will see that times of challenge present some of the best opportunities to transform fear of failure into joy for learning.

But this boy's mother saw through the eyes of a coach. Rather than chastising and punishing him, she kept her cool. Together, she and her son got down on the floor and turned the mistake into an opportunity for a science lesson. She showed her boy how the milk flowed into puddles and spread across the floor in a definite pattern. They examined the carton and tried to figure out why the carton had split upon contact with the floor in the way it had. They talked about why drinking from the carton is unsanitary and can spread disease. As they cleaned up the mess she taught him about absorption. All the while she asked him questions that caused him to think. Gently, she helped him understand that she didn't want him to repeat this mistake, and even more, she wanted him to learn something from every experience.

Coaching is less about catching others doing things wrong and chastising them for their mistakes, and more about helping them see ways they can use those experiences to improve and grow. There is immense potential in everyone that is stifled most often by fear. Through the eyes of a coach you will see that times of challenge present some of the best opportunities to transform fear of failure into joy for learning. Nothing is more fulfilling than guiding this transformation in everyone you touch.

Meet Coach John Wooden–a shining example of humility, integrity, and balance.
We can all aspire to his life's principles.

Tapping Into the Wisdom of a Coaching Legend: Heart to Heart with John Wooden

The philosophies and strategies in this book work! They strengthen your family, improve your business, and add immeasurable satisfaction, energy, and love to your life. The proof will become readily apparent as you put these ideas into action in your life. Yet, you may hesitate to try the strategies until you've seen visible proof of the results generated by those who have already applied the concepts. A man who personified the best in coaching was John Wooden, the most successful basketball coach in college history. I had the opportunity to interview Coach Wooden and found that his example provides a vivid demonstration of the legacy that can be created by living according to the principles and strategies you find through the eyes of a coach.

For most of my life I have followed John Wooden's career as a coach and a leader. It had been my dream to spend some time with him since I was twelve years old. He has always embodied integrity and class. His peace of mind, humility, and graciousness are so genuine that it is easy to forget he accomplished more in his highly competitive field than any other by far.

In his final twelve years at UCLA, Coach Wooden's teams won a staggering total of ten National Championships. No other coach has won more than four. He is the only individual to be elected to the College Basketball Hall of Fame as both a player and a coach. He is one of a kind, a true legend.

Yet, it is not so much *what* Coach Wooden accomplished that is the measure of his greatness. It is *how* he achieved his success. As unparalleled as his basketball coaching record is, he was an even better husband and father. John Wooden always remembered that he coached people first, basketball second. That understanding is pivotal to see through the eyes of a coach. Whether your arena is athletics, business, education, or parenting, the prime focus of your coaching is ultimately the human spirit.

John Wooden always remembered that he coached people first, basketball second.

When I decided to arrange an interview with Coach Wooden, I had clear outcomes in mind. First and foremost, I was determined to be a sponge—to gain deep understanding of the basic philosophies, beliefs, and strategies that he lives by, and to share that information with others. Each of us has the opportunity to positively impact the quality of life in our families, our work environments, and our communities. By modeling a coach of John Wooden's caliber, we will gain insights that will help us become increasingly successful in our careers and in our lives.

Coach Wooden has always loved poetry and philosophical quotations. He has attached so much meaning to several key bits of verse that, taken together, they portray a sense of his true character. I thought it appropriate to build this bonus section around some of the most revealing of these quotes. If you're like me, some of the ideas will capture your imagination and become cornerstones of your own coaching philosophy and strategy. You'll discover that the foundational beliefs that have guided John Wooden are clear, simple, and available for you to emulate and internalize. Model the wisdom of the "Wizard of Westwood" and become the leader and coach you were meant to be!

"True happiness comes from the things that can't be taken away."

When I first arrived for our interview, Coach Wooden greeted me at the security gate and we walked together into his apartment. He lives quite modestly, as material wealth has never been a primary priority in his life. When he excused himself for a moment, I took advantage of the opportunity to look about the room for clues to the priorities that motivate Coach Wooden. Everywhere I turned, I saw pictures of family—children, grandchildren, and great-grandchildren. Conspicuously absent were the hundreds of awards he had won over the years. Indeed, the 'trophies' that have real meaning to him are his family mementos and his books. He is a ravenous reader with scores of books of poetry, novels, biographies, and spiritual volumes filling his shelves. For just a moment before he joined me, I allowed myself to reflect upon this special opportunity. Here I was, in John Wooden's living room,

Indeed, the 'trophies' that have real meaning to him are his family mementos and his books.

about to learn all I could from the coach who set the standard for all others. Wow, what a moment! In the next hour and a half, I would begin to discover what specifically generated this man's unparalleled success.

Let's begin with the foundation. What is it that is so unique about John Wooden? As I drove home deep in thought after the interview, the answer came clearly into focus. I have never met a man who is more centered on his priorities. He has so internalized his coaching philosophy in the form of quotes, poems, and creeds that he repeats and affirms it every single day through conversations, writings, speeches, prayer, and his disciplined thoughts. The long-term impact of this practice was immense. Over time these affirmations combined to create a dynamic composite of his beliefs.

I have never met a man who is more centered on his priorities.

The cornerstone of Coach Wooden's philosophy was a simple creed given to him by his father on the day John graduated from his one-room country grade school. Coach Wooden carried the creed with him in one form or another from that day forward:

1. **Be true to yourself.**
2. **Make each day your masterpiece.**
3. **Help others.**
4. **Drink deeply from good books, especially the Bible.**
5. **Make friendship a fine art.**
6. **Build a shelter against a rainy day.**
7. **Pray for guidance; count and give thanks for your blessings every day.**

The creed clearly defines the essence of John Wooden's life. To live according to this creed is to move swiftly and purposefully along the pathway to true success.

Early in our interview, I asked him about his approach to a season, to practice sessions, and to games. *Balance* and *preparation* were the overriding themes in his answer. He is a long-term thinker who uses the short-term to assess his direction and fine-tune his strategy. Three of his ever-present quotes illustrate his philosophy:

"Failure to prepare is preparing to fail."

"Be quick, but never hurry."

"Learn as if you were to live forever; live as if you were to die tomorrow."

Coach Wooden's strategy during the off-season demonstrated his dedication to preparation and ongoing improvement. As soon as the college season was completed, he selected a single topic to study in great depth over the subsequent six months. In his early years, he chose physical or strategic aspects of the game of basketball, like rebounding or zone defenses. In later years, he chose more psychological elements of the sport such as pregame mental preparation or visualization. During the off-season, he devoured every piece of information he could find about his selected topic. He interviewed fellow coaches to identify fine details that enhanced his knowledge and understanding. There was no satisfying his voracious appetite for learning.

Not content to simply gather information, he went much further and constructed a "composite" of the most

During the off-season, he devoured every piece of information he could find about his selected topic.

important distinctions he accumulated from his study. By applying himself creatively in this way, he prepared himself to effectively teach the new ideas. He understood that mastery requires proactive involvement and application rather than passive study.

Coach Wooden's commitment to learning contributed greatly to his humility. He always knew there was more to discover. One of my favorite of his common sense quotes sums up his "uncommon" philosophy: **"It's what you learn after you know everything that makes the difference."**

Coach Wooden's commitment to learning contributed greatly to his humility.

Ultimately, those who constantly look for finer and finer distinctions, and then use the increased knowledge as teachers, coaches, and practitioners will soar to the tops of their fields. John Wooden, the most successful basketball coach in history, remained constantly open to learn from every source possible.

To achieve coaching excellence, you must challenge yourself to be a dedicated lifetime student in your chosen art.

"Success accompanies attention to little details. It is this that makes for the difference between champion and near champion."

Coach Wooden considered his ability to organize practices one of his primary strengths. He was known for running practices that were relatively short and meticulously planned. Every moment of every practice involved movement and purpose. Practice started on time and ended on time. Players moved in units from drill to drill with the emphasis on repetition, repetition, repetition. By practicing fundamentals constantly and with great concentration, good judgment and precision execution became automatic.

Over the years, he became convinced that every detail was important. A classic example of this extraordinary attention to detail was his annual training session on *socks*. Coach Wooden believed no player is better than his feet. If you had blisters or sores, they could easily slow you down at crucial moments. Consequently, each season he gave his players a detailed, step-by-step demonstration about how to put on their socks so they could avoid the wrinkles that create blisters. Wooden's attention to detail made a lasting positive impression on his players and students. They knew that if there was an edge to be gained, their coach would find it.

Apply a level of detail to your work by planning your meetings, training sessions, and presentations with careful consideration of the small touches that can make big differences.

You can apply this level of detail to your work by planning your meetings, training sessions, and presentations with careful consideration of the small touches that can make big differences. By developing this heightened level of concentration as a coach, you will create an example that will translate into positive habits within your team.

Coach Wooden made it a must to end each workout on a happy note. In every practice there were positives and negatives, just as there are in every day. He recognized that what you focus on determines your attitude. Many people cling to the painful or negative experiences in each day. By ending every practice and game on an upbeat note, Coach Wooden helped his players enjoy their experience and look forward with positive anticipation to their next workout.

Coach Wooden was extremely dedicated to integrating the day to day progress and experience of his team. He kept personal notebooks that he updated constantly. One contained detailed statistical records of his team's performance. The other was a listing of all the drills and practices his players had completed during the season. These notebooks enabled Coach Wooden to tell you precisely what his players did during any practice from 1949 through 1975. He could enumerate each player's statistics from every practice during that same span. But even more important than recording the information was his regular practice of using it. He measured and assessed these records daily in his preparation for practices and games. His practices were radically different between 1949 when he began at UCLA and 1975 when he retired. However, the changes from year to year were subtle. It was through his steadfast dedication to measuring, recording, and integrating that he was able to keep his changes moving positively in the direction he sought.

Coach Wooden was extremely dedicated to integrating the day to day progress and experience of his team.

"It's amazing how much can be accomplished when no one cares who gets the credit."

This quote captures the heart of John Wooden's vision of team centered around unselfishness, camaraderie, and united purpose. Coach Wooden's UCLA squads were the epitome of this team concept. His belief system concerning team began with a core conviction:

"A man may make mistakes, but he isn't a failure until he starts blaming someone else."

Blaming others takes away your focus from the one element in human performance that you control: *you*. It dissipates your energy and destroys teamwork. This same basic tenet is true in a family, in a company, and within yourself. Coach Wooden thrived on accepting the responsibility for his team in good times and bad. And he taught his players daily to accept their responsibility to themselves and their team. To Coach Wooden, personal responsibility is a fundamental gift from God.

Wooden taught that every member of the unit, from the players to the coaches, trainers, and student managers—everybody—plays an essential role. Unselfishness was a trait he absolutely insisted upon. To him, the greatest privilege his athletes had was to practice, and the next was to play in the games. If a player put himself before the team, he would remove those privileges. He said that the bench was sometimes a coach's best friend. When asked to characterize what made for a great team player, he thought about his answer carefully and replied: "All of the great team players at UCLA were different in many ways. Yet, in one way they were the same. Each drove himself to be the best he could be—*always in relation to the team.* They weren't motivated by personal statistics or awards. The only credit they truly valued was credit for the team."

We are all part of a team. As a coach you can instill tremendous devotion and mutual support by helping every team member know that they are important.

To Coach Wooden, personal responsibility is a fundamental gift from God.

Recognize and acknowledge the sometimes subtle, behind-the-scenes examples of unselfish contributions that could easily go unnoticed, yet make overall success and improvement possible.

"Be more concerned with your character than your reputation, because your character is what you really are, while your reputation is merely what others think you are."

They weren't motivated by personal statistics or awards. The only credit they truly valued was credit for the team.

When you meet Coach Wooden you discover what true integrity is. He speaks softly and exudes great gentleness, yet his power is unmistakable. It is immediately apparent that he is neither motivated by the need for approval nor to control others, but rather to serve. Integrity is not a technique. It is genuineness of spirit. When you connect with others, whether customers, teammates, friends, or family, your true internal motivations cannot be hidden in the long run. Honor your character rather than worrying about your reputation, and you will exemplify the kind of leadership that brings out the best in all you touch.

"Success is peace of mind, which is a direct result of self-satisfaction in knowing you did your best to become the best that you are capable of becoming."

In twenty-seven years as the coach of UCLA basketball, John Wooden never used the words *winning* or *losing* when speaking with his teams. Both, he believed, were out of our direct control. Instead, he sought to ingrain the above definition of success within himself and his teams. The implications of this philosophy are enormous. By living according to this view, you put yourself at the cause and not the effect: The control and responsibility for your success lies within yourself at every moment, and in every instance.

Internalization of this definition of success leads away from external comparison and evaluation. Instead of driving himself and each of his players toward external goals, Coach Wooden constantly focused on assisting each of his players to discover his personal best, always within the bigger framework of the team. In this way, it was not the championships which determined his success as a coach in his own mind, it was the inner knowledge that he had done his absolute best to help each player approach his full potential.

The control and responsibility for your success lies within yourself at every moment, and in every instance.

At the end of our interview I asked John Wooden what mattered the most to him as a coach. He asked me to wait while he went into another room to get something that would give me a better answer than any words he could muster. He came back in a moment with a small tape player and an audiocassette of a song that one of his former players had adapted from Bette Midler's *The Wind Beneath My Wings* to thank the man who had meant so much to him and so many others. As we listened together, tears streamed down both of our cheeks, and he told me this was worth more than any award, trophy, or championship. To make a difference in others' lives is the greatest of all gifts and the driving purpose behind all great coaches. Your reward is to watch them soar and to know that you are always with them, encouraging, believing, and serving—the ever-present wind beneath their wings.

Honor your character rather than worrying about your reputation, and you will exemplify the kind of leadership that brings out the best in all you touch.

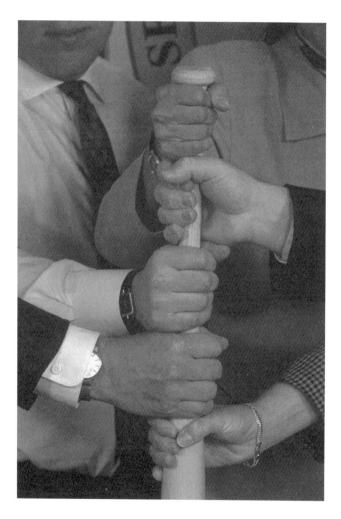

Just like children, big kids (adults) love to play. When you involve your teammates in games, they can discover opportunities, lessons, and breakthroughs that have eluded them in the all too serious "real" world.

bonus section two

Games to Bring Your Team Together:

Game #1: The Blind Date

There are tremendous secrets in this simple, fun game. Here's the way it works: Have each player find a buddy. Hand out blindfolds to each player. Bandannas work beautifully. Each player will serve as the "guide" for five minutes, and will also be the "blind date" for five minutes. Give the following instructions at this point:

"When I set you free, you can go anywhere you like during the blind date. At the five-minute mark, switch roles, wherever you are. If you were the guide, you will become the blind date, and vice versa. Here are three guidelines:

"1. Help your date discover more of the world than he or she ever would have with his or her eyes open.

"2. Make it incredibly fun, creative, and vibrant: a truly enriching experience.

"3. Take great care of your date.

"GO!"

Note: During the game, turn up your alertness as the coach—watch, listen, and play. Call out "Switch!" at the five-minute mark and give time-remaining announcements with two and then one minute to go.

To help the team integrate the experience when they're done, tell them, "Thank your buddy! How many of you had a great time on your blind date? Great! How many really enjoyed being blindfolded? (These are the *adventurers!*) How many really liked being the guide? (These are the *controllers!*) How many enjoyed both roles?"

Now you will help all the participants discover the secrets and powerful principles at work in this game. Your role as coach is to facilitate a question-and-answer session that will foster tremendous learning. Have fun as you guide the process and be sure to illuminate each key learning point. Following are some questions you can include:

Have fun as you guide the process and be sure to illuminate each key learning point.

1. "What was it like for you to be blindfolded?" Listen and enjoy the responses. Many will say they felt frightened and tentative—as if they were about to fall into a forty-foot hole at any moment. *Key Learning Point:* Being blindfolded was about trust. Every participant had the opportunity to experience whether or not they fully trusted—at least in this context. Also ask, "Who did you have to trust?" As this question sets in, it becomes apparent that the blind dates must trust both the guide and themselves. In fact, before the guide can begin to create a rich experience for the blind date, the blindfolded person must let go and trust their guide, or the date will never unfold.

2. "How many of you found yourself becoming less fearful and tentative as you went along?

What happened to your experience as you trusted more?" *Key Learning Point:* The more you trust, the richer your experience. Your senses come alive and you notice much more of the world. By taking away the dominant sense of sight, the other senses become more acute. For example, the most underused sense is hearing. When we are in a conversation, what are most of us actually doing when the other person is speaking? The truth is, we are usually formulating our response. This keeps us from fully listening. People who make the most of their potential share a special characteristic—they have a heightened level of alertness. They use more of their senses to gather information and discover solutions and connections. We all have huge potential for this. One of the special secrets in this game is an "aha" about the benefit of increasing our alertness.

People who make the most of their potential share a special characteristic–they have a heightened level of alertness.

3. "When you were tentative and frightened as you began your time being blindfolded, what did you notice?" *Key Learning Point:* When we are in the state of not trusting, we only notice our fear—everything else is blocked out.

4. "What was it like for you to be the guide?" Once again, listen and enjoy the responses. *Key Learning Point:* For most, being the guide is about responsibility. What would happen if each participant in the game accepted the level of responsibility with their teammates at work and at home that they willingly shouldered in this game? One of the great gifts of this game is to feel that level of responsibility for a teammate.

After this point has been made, ask how many guides focused their responsibility more on guideline #2 ("make it incredibly fun, creative, and vibrant: a truly enriching experience") and how many focused more of their responsibility on #3 ("take great care of them"). *Key Learning Point:* Where you focus your responsibility as a coach has a tremendous effect on the results you generate. If you focus too much on #3, eventually you teach and coach dependence. As a coach, one of your primary goals is to instill *self*-motivation. For example, as a parent, somewhere along the road it is critical that your children learn to believe in themselves, to develop their own purpose, and to feel inspired about their lives. This requires a shift in the focus of your responsibility from #3 to #2.

When you step forward to serve others, which is true leadership, you can't help but grow!

5. "When you think back to your experience as the guide, what happened to your discovery of the world?" *Key Learning Point:* When people focus on being guides, they discover far more of the world than had they not accepted that responsibility. When you accept the responsibility to enrich another's experience, *you can't help but enrich your own!* This is the hidden gift of leadership and service. In other words, when you step forward to serve others, which is true leadership, you can't help but grow! Yes!!

6. "How did you help your date discover more of the world than with their eyes open?" Listen carefully to the responses. Most will say they described things and had their date touch objects. Once you've listened to these responses ask this key question: "How many of you spent at least half your time as the guide asking your date questions?" You'll see few hands go up! *Key Learning Point:* This points out a paradox of leadership. When we strive to take care of our teammates, we can easily get caught up in thinking we're supposed to do everything for them. We fall into the trap of telling instead of asking questions. When we tell instead of ask, what do we take away? The answer is *discovery!*

When you think about it, aren't there some great questions you could ask a blind date? For example, "What color do you think this is?" Or, "We have one minute left. How would you find your way back to the room?" Wouldn't that create a totally different experience? The key is not that the blindfolded partner answers these questions correctly; it's that by asking the questions you have helped them access a part of their insight and intuition they could well have missed.

During the blind date, both participants are one hundred percent present with each other.

7. "How many of you felt a real connection with your partner in this game?" *Key Learning Point:* Though initially the blind date appears to be a game about trust, it is ultimately a powerful example of the importance of being fully present. You can't get away with not being present on this date or you'll run your partner into a wall! The truth is, during the blind date both participants are one hundred percent present with each other. They are not thinking about yesterday or the meetings they have next week. The outcome of this presence is wonderful connection, a feeling of closeness, trust, and importance that is unmistakable. This game gives each participant a true experience of the message in Chapter 10: *The Truly Precious Present.*

Over the years I have come to view the blind date as one of the most valuable exercises you could ever experience because we are almost always in a state of either being guides or blindfolded. When we work with customers, teammates, or family members, we are often seeking to be great guides. We want to help them because we have more experience or knowledge in a particular area. They are somewhat "blindfolded" because they do not have much experience. At other times, it is just the opposite. We need to be guided because often the greatest obstacle to discovering the truth is the belief that we already know it. The principles about being present, trusting, asking instead of telling, turning up our alertness, serving, and responsibility are enormously important elements in building great teams. This game helps you bring these ideas to life in thirty minutes of fun and awakening that can save you months of struggle!

When we work with customers, teammates, or family members, we are often seeking to be great guides.

Game #2: The Hula Hoop Relay

This hilarious, energized game is unmatched when it comes to helping a team learn to beat with one heart. For this game, you'll need two large-sized hula hoops (available at any major toy store), a stopwatch or a watch with a second hand, and a minimum of twelve participants. Here are the instructions:

1. Have everyone hold hands, forming the group into a connected circle.

2. Announce, "This is a game of *speed*!" Then repeat to the group with great energy, "This is a game of . . . ?" The team will call out the word *speed*! If they are not loud enough, repeat it again!

3. Next announce that there are only two simple rules to the hula hoop relay: "You may not let go of one another's hands, and you are to act as a *team*!"

4. Decide where you want to start the hoops (one hoop directly across the circle from where you place the first). You unlock the hands of the two people at the spot where you have chosen to start the first hoop, set the hoop over their hands, and relock them. Do the same on the opposite side of the circle with the second hoop. Once both hoops are positioned, announce, "This is a game of what?" They will call back, *"Speed!"*

5. Announce while using physical gestures to demonstrate: "When I say go, the clock will start. This hoop must go this way (clockwise) around the circle." Then rush over to the other hoop on the opposite side of the circle and continue, "And this hoop must go this way (counterclockwise). When each hoop has made it all the way around the circle and returned to where it started, the clock will stop. This is a game of what?" *("Speed!")* "You may not let go of each others' whats?" *("Hands!")* "You are to act as a what?" *("Team!")* "Ready, set, go!" (Be sure to start your stopwatch or note the time carefully on your second hand).

As they begin, just step back and observe. Listen to the level of their cheering (if any) and enthusiasm. Watch for

The principles about being present, trusting, asking instead of telling, turning up our alertness, serving, and responsibility are enormously important elements in building great teams.

the level of energy. Are they really going for it? Or are some casually making their way through? Notice whether they physically help one another. Also, is there anyone who keeps on trying despite getting a bit tangled up? Turn up your powers of observation so that your upcoming facilitation and integration is right on target.

When they have managed to get the hoops around the circle and back to their starting points, stop the clock. Enthusiastically announce their time. They will applaud. You can quip, " That's what I like about you. You have no idea if that's a good time or not, but you applaud anyway!"

Turn up your powers of observation so that your upcoming facilitation and integration is right on target.

Now begin to really bring this game to life. You will now raise their standards. Simply say, "I *know* you can improve your time. This time, your goal is ——————." (A good rule of thumb is to set a time that is fifteen seconds faster for every twenty participants than the previous time. Thus, if you had forty players, set a time of thirty seconds faster and forty-five seconds faster if you have sixty participants, etc.) With great conviction, say, "I know you can do it! How many of you believe me?" (This should be energized—have them respond by raising their hands and cheering yes!). Then continue, "If we're going to achieve our new goal, we'll need to act more as a team. *How could we be more of a team?*"

You are looking for three key principles to come out here:

1. Cheer and support each other! Odds are, they were fairly quiet the first time through the game. They might have cheered only when they got through the first crossing of the hoops, and perhaps right at the end. Give examples of the power of cheering and supporting to lift performance. I tell the story of the Winter Olympics and the U.S. Ice Hockey team in Lake Placid, New York in 1980. A group of American college kids pulled off an unbelievable upset by beating the Russian team made up of the greatest players in the world. What kind of crowd was in Lake Placid that day? A totally psyched up, incredibly loud U.S. crowd. It made a huge difference. Ask your participants how they can apply the principle of cheering and supporting each other in their work and at home.

2. Help each other! The key learning point here is to overcome the that's-not-my-job/department syndrome. If you see an opportunity to help a teammate through a fresh idea, suggestion, or action, go for it! It's also vital that the receiver be open to the help and not push it away. *Key question:* "What would happen if an atmosphere was created where help was welcome, both to offer and receive?" The team would soar!

3. Energy! This is a great place to reinforce the importance of energy. Ask, "At what energy level on a ten-point scale did the team operate as they moved through the hoops first time? What would happen if everyone elevated their energy level this second time at least two full points?"

You're now ready for round two. Keep the energy high and set the hoops at two new points opposite one another. Point out the direction each is to go. Ask them to repeat their goal for this time through: "Remember: Cheer and

"If we're going to achieve our new goal, we'll need to act more as a team. How could we be more of a team?"

support each other, help each other, and *energy!* ready, set, *go!*"

This time through you'll see heightened energy, more fun, and, very likely, considerable performance improvement. In many cases they will surpass the goal you've set for them. If not, odds are that they simply were so pumped up, they got a little extra tangled. Nineteen times out of twenty, however, they will have improved tons. When they finish, celebrate!

Ask, "What was different this time? How did it feel to have more energy?" Bring home the truth that by cheering and supporting each other, helping each other, and raising their energy they not only improved tremendously, they had more fun doing it! The same is true in the workplace and with your real life teams.

Bring home the truth that by cheering and supporting each other, helping each other, and raising their energy they not only improved tremendously, they had more fun doing it!

Now you're ready for round three. Repeat the three principles they've learned about being more of a team—cheering and supporting each other, helping each other, and raising their energy—and let them know that up to now you've given them no time to strategize. Announce with great enthusiasm that you are certain they can complete the game this time in less than thirty seconds! They may have gone from two minutes and thirty seconds in round one to one minute and twenty seconds in round two. You are really raising the bar with this goal of less than thirty seconds for round three. Ask how many believe you. Watch carefully here. You will likely see far less certainty now compared to when you set their new goal after round one. The difference in energy will be apparent. This new goal seems out of reach to most.

Now give them two minutes to strategize and practice. Notice whether they come together to find solutions or if they break off into cliques and subgroups. Is everyone involved in looking for winning strategies, or are some off on their own, not participating? Who are the dominators, the ones who hold back, or those who check out altogether? Once again, your alertness as you watch the process unfold will make all the difference in the impact of your facilitation and integration of the game.

Ask them if they came up with a solution that everybody knew and agreed upon.

After two minutes stop them on deadline. Have them come together very close around you. Ask them if they came up with a solution that everybody knew and agreed upon. "What was the two minutes like?" This is a great opportunity for you to teach key learning points about meetings, the power of questions, brainstorming, and transforming all players into full participants and eager team players.

Here are some Key Learning Points they should get from your discussion:

1. The two-minute, frenzied strategy session was like a lot of business meetings—lots of talking and little listening. Ask the team what the most prevalent challenges with many meetings are. They will come up with all sorts of points which directly relate to what they have just experienced. For example, a few people dominate everyone else, ideas are squelched rather than considered, when the meeting is over there is less clarity than when it started, and no one seems to have a solid idea of what to do next.

2. Explain that in most meetings, there tend to be people who become "dominators." These are the people who jump right to the front with energy and determination to give instructions. At this point surprise everyone by thanking the dominators for at least being eager to put themselves out there to make something happen. Then encourage them to expand their horizons, because there is almost always another group of people present who we'll call "holder-backers."

They'll recognize that holder-backers many times have tremendous ideas and insights.

Ask the team who often has the best ideas. Boom! They'll recognize that holder-backers many times have tremendous ideas and insights. Why? Because they take in everything—watching, listening, connecting. Dominators only notice their own idea and block everything else out. The problem with holder-backers is they won't step forward with their ideas. They hold them in. Why do holder-backers keep their ideas locked inside? Because some time in their past they were humiliated or stepped on for offering some different idea. They learned it was safer to keep quiet. If holder-backers withdraw further, they can slip into becoming "checker outers." These are the individuals who keep completely to themselves, who will no longer even be involved through their powers of observation.

At this point, encourage everyone to focus on becoming "bringer-outers!" Dominators can look around and notice the tuned-in holder-backers and quietly ask them if they have any ideas. Holder-backers can also get creative about ways they can feel comfortable to bring their ideas to the table. For example, they can find the nearest dominator and express the idea to that individual, who will then bring it to the group. When everyone looks to be a bringer-outer, you will have a team running on all cylinders.

This is a great place to introduce the Team Possibility format, a simple and effective method for getting a tremendous amount done in meetings. Here is how it works:

1. Create your agenda as a series of *questions.*

2. The Team Possibility meeting is organized into a three-step process: brainstorming, prioritizing, and action commitments.

When everyone looks to be a bringer-outer, you will have a team running on all cylinders.

Brainstorming is fast-paced with no assessment. Every idea is recorded. With such a welcoming and open atmosphere, an incredible number of ideas will be generated in a short time.

During prioritization, the team will determine which ideas and solutions they feel most beneficial and important to put into action.

Finally, during the last portion of the meeting, the team members will make individual action commitments. These are simply who will do what, by when.

Benefits: The clock is your friend in the Team Possibility meeting. You use it to create energy. Everyone knows the time frame is short and fast-paced. This elevates the level of concentration and alertness. Everyone involved in the Team Possibility meeting is involved and active from the opening brainstorming. All ideas are recorded and honored because there is no assessment during the creative session. Each individual knows he or she has the opportunity to be heard and to contribute. You will accomplish more in a forty-five-minute Team Possibility meeting than in typical two-hour sessions. Most exciting, everyone knows their next step when they walk out of the meeting.

Explain to your hula hoop team that the two-minute strategy session could have been run as a mini–Team Possibility meeting. They could have had one-minute for brainstorming ideas—quick, concise, clear. Then they could have used the second minute to prioritize—deciding which strategy to implement. Because everyone must participate in the relay, the action commitments are already determined.

During prioritiza-tion, the team will determine which ideas and solutions they feel most beneficial and impor-tant to put into action.

At this point, you can run a quick Team-Possibility session with the hula hoopers. Let them brainstorm ideas and agree on a plan for round three. When they're ready let them go for it! At least two strategies will enable the team to easily complete the game in less than the thirty-second goal you have set for them. One strategy is to move the group instead of the hoop. This means that all members of the team run in a clockwise circle one full revolution when you say go, and then immediately reverse and run a full counterclockwise circle. With this strategy, the hoops stay with the same people all the way around, yet they make their two full circles. I'll leave the second and other strategies for you and your team to discover!

To wrap things up, have everyone thank at least two of their hula hoop buddies and sit down together to integrate the game. Start by re-emphasizing the importance and value of the principles they successfully used to be more of a team— cheering and supporting each other, helping each other, and raising their energy—when they improved from round one to round two. These principles alone make an enormous difference.

Next, explain that the game also provides an ideal example of how to generate remarkable growth in your team. There is a four-step process to initiate unstoppable improvement:

Goal setting is an imagination game.

1. Raise the bar.
2. Heighten your alertness.
3. Change your belief about what's possible for you and your team.
4. Find and implement a better strategy.

A simple review of the game reveals how this four-step process comes into play. The first thing I did in the hula hoop relay when we finished round one was to raise the bar. I said, "I *know* you can improve your time to ———!" and then watched closely for their response when I asked if they really believed they could achieve the new goal.

Later when we integrated the game I asked participants where that new standard had come from. Immediately they answered correctly—I snatched the goal out of the ether. I had a bit of experience to guide me, but basically the process of raising the bar was no more than making stuff up! This is an important realization for them as coaches. Goal setting is an imagination game.

When I raised the bar again by setting a new goal time

before the third round, I again asked the team how many of them *believed* they could achieve the new level. At that point it was crucial for me to tune in as a leader and notice the level of their belief (mainly by observing their body language) because during integration I asked the group, "How many of you felt a major decline in your confidence about achieving your third round goal?" I got lots of hands and nods of agreement. Then I asked, "How many of you have ever had the bar raised by a manager or leader, but didn't believe you could achieve the new standard? In fact, you may have felt you were already giving everything you had just to perform at your present level." Finally when I asked, "How does it make you feel when someone raises the bar for you, and you already *feel* like you're giving your best?' They answered, "angry, disillusioned, like giving up, frustrated, defeated, unappreciated..."

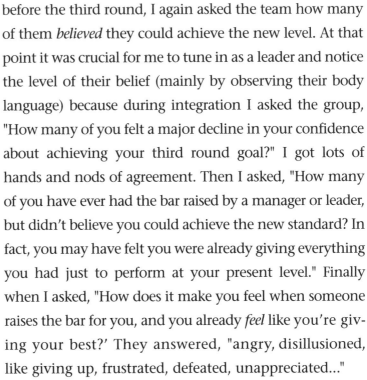

The process of raising the bar was no more than making stuff up!

That's why, without changing disempowering beliefs about what's possible for you and your team, raising the bar will have the opposite impact on improvement you desire. And, without heightening your alertness, you won't be able to accurately gauge the level of belief. It's not enough to ask the question, "How many of you believe you can do it?" You must heighten your alertness as a leader, both in the way you observe others and yourself. You must become clear whether your team is simply giving you lip service telling you what you want to hear, or if they truly have a high level of belief.

The hula hoop relay provides a great example. When I asked the team how many believed they could improve markedly from round one to round two, the response was positive and unanimous. All could feel the energy and confidence. However, when I told them they could improve to less than thirty seconds in round three (raising the bar far higher), I observed far less certainty in their response. They may have said yes, but their body language expressed lots of doubt. When asked later if they felt the decline in their positive belief, their lack of confidence was obvious to them. This brings out a key responsibility as a coach. When you see and feel that the team's belief is wavering with doubt and uncertainty, you must help them elevate their faith.

When you see and feel that the team's belief is wavering with doubt and uncertainty, you must help them elevate their faith.

How do you instill greater certainty into the hearts of your teammates? Start by asking your team, "What is a belief?" Let the question sink in for just a moment or two, then ask another question. "How many of you believe something today that you didn't believe five years ago?" You'll see virtually every hand go up. Follow with, "So the first thing we know about beliefs is that they can do what?" The group will respond with a resounding, "Change!" Now ask for the definition of a belief again. They will give you some good answers. Enjoy them and build upon their responses. Offer the statement that a belief is nothing but a feeling of certainty about what something is or means. This feeling of certainty is supported by experiences or references that are real or vividly imagined.

Now ask, "So if you are a leader seeking to help elevate your team's level of belief in themselves, or you want to change your own disempowering belief, how can you go about it effectively? In other words, when you see your team lacking faith, what can you do to help them change?"

Listen at this point for some great ideas. Encourage the team to put those ideas into action. Here are a few key learning points to add if they are not offered by the team:

1. Your own enthusiasm and level of belief can be powerful. Be a strong positive Pygmalion.

If you are a leader seeking to help elevate your team's level of belief in themselves, how can you go about it effectively?

2. Breaking the new standard you have set into smaller chunks can make a big difference. The team may be able to see themselves twenty-five percent of the way to the bar, but not all the way. As soon as they see themselves making some improvement, they create momentum and begin to reel the goal in.

3. Ask them to think of a time when they achieved something about which they originally felt doubtful and uncertain. By asking them about their real experience of triumph in the face of a major challenge, you help them become fully associated to their ability to exceed their own expectations. They access the same resources and energy that served them earlier.

4. Use a surprise metaphor or game like the F-card to help them see there is more than meets the eye. The same is true of their own potential.

Once you have observed that the level of belief in their ability to reach the new goal is strong, the final step in unstoppable improvement is to find and implement a better strategy. It's critical that the belief is solidified first, however, or strategic vision is severely limited.

End by once again identifying the hula hoop relay as a great example of the unstoppable improvement process. Ask, "Think back now and imagine if we had just done one round of the hula hoop relay. What would be have missed? How much of our ability and potential may have been left untapped? Odds are, we would have had no idea how rapidly and dramatically we could improve our performance." That's why it so pivotal to ensure that your team knows that the possibility for unstoppable improvement is ever-present.

By asking them about their real experience of triumph in the face of a major challenge, you help them become fully associated to their ability to exceed their own expectations.